Telling Our Stories

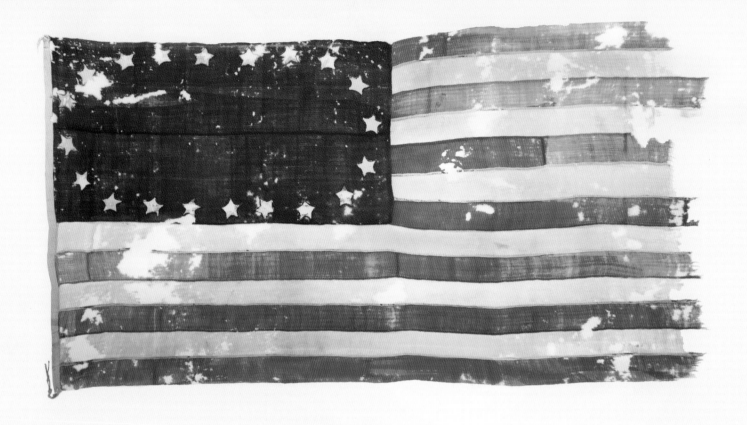

United States flag, handspun cotton thread, 1818. Mississippi became the twentieth state on December 10, 1817. Congress adopted the 20-star flag in 1818, as part of a new law that added a star on the Fourth of July following the admission of each new state. The 20-star flag served as the US standard through July 3, 1819, when a twenty-first star was added for Illinois. Evidence indicates that this flag flew on a Massachusetts ship.

Telling Our Stories

MUSEUM OF MISSISSIPPI HISTORY

and

MISSISSIPPI CIVIL RIGHTS MUSEUM

Mississippi Department of Archives and History

UNIVERSITY PRESS OF MISSISSIPPI / JACKSON

www.upress.state.ms.us

The University Press of Mississippi is a member of the Association of
American University Presses.
Excerpt of "For My People" from *This Is My Century: New and Collected Poems* by Margaret Walker
(Athens: University of Georgia Press, 1989). Reprinted by permission.

Illustrated artifacts and documents are from the collection of Mississippi Department of
Archives and History unless otherwise noted.
Managing Editor: Amanda Lyons
Editor: Robin C. Dietrick
Book Design: Peter D. Halverson
Photographs by Christina Cannon Boteler / Christina Foto unless otherwise noted.
Photograph by James Patterson: ii
Photographs by Jonathan Thomas: 29, 55, 81, 85
Photographs by Mississippi Department of Archives and History: viii, 16, 37, 43, 53, 55, 57, 60, 63, 66,
68–70, 74, 79, 82, 88, 89, 91, 92, 102, 112, 119, 127, 130, 132, 134, 148, 153, 154, 160, and 165

First printing 2017
∞

Library of Congress Cataloging-in-Publication Data

Names: Lyons, Amanda (Historian), editor. | Dietrick, Robin C., 1978– editor. | Boteler, Christina
    Cannon, photographer. | Mississippi. Department of Archives and History.
Title: Telling our stories : Museum of Mississippi History and Mississippi Civil Rights Museum /
    Mississippi Department of Archives and History ; managing editor Amanda Lyons ;
    editor Robin C. Dietrick ; photographs by Christina Cannon Boteler.
Description: Jackson : University Press of Mississippi, [2017] | Includes index. | Description based on
    print version record and CIP data provided by publisher; resource not viewed.
Identifiers: LCCN 2017010838 (print) | LCCN 2017012572 (ebook) | ISBN 9781496813497 (epub single)
    | ISBN 9781496813503 (epub institutional) | ISBN 9781496813510 (pdf single) | ISBN 9781496813527
    (pdf institutional) | ISBN 9781496813480 (cloth : alk. paper) | ISBN 9781496813534 (mobi)
Subjects: LCSH: Museum of Mississippi History. | Mississippi Civil Rights Museum. | Historical
    museums—Mississippi—Jackson. | Civil rights—Museums—Mississippi—Jackson.
Classification: LCC F338 (ebook) | LCC F338 .T45 2017 (print) | DDC 069.09762/51—dc23
LC record available at https://lccn.loc.gov/2017010838

British Library Cataloging-in-Publication Data available

This book was made possible by the generous support of Baptist Health Systems.

MUSEUM OF MISSISSIPPI HISTORY

Contents

MISSISSIPPI CIVIL RIGHTS MUSEUM

Fragment of boundary marker, cut into tree by William L. S. Deering in 1832. The United States dispatched surveyors to record Mississippi's growing boundaries. This boundary marker indicated the line between Noxubee and Kemper Counties, both of which came into the state's possession through forced Choctaw cessions. The fragment bears the reverse of the letter "R," part of the original survey record carved into the post oak tree.

Foreword

HALEY BARBOUR AND REUBEN V. ANDERSON

IN DECEMBER 2017, the state of Mississippi opened the 2 Mississippi Museums in celebration of its bicentennial. Not since the construction of the New Capitol in 1903 has the state completed a historic building project of this magnitude. The architectural design and scale of the building are monumental, but the true significance lies in the vision behind the project. Standing side by side on LeFleur's Bluff in downtown Jackson, the Museum of Mississippi History and the Mississippi Civil Rights Museum tell our state's stories in all their complexity. The Civil Rights Museum will be the first state-operated civil rights museum in the country.

The 2 Mississippi Museums started as separate projects. The Mississippi Department of Archives and History had been planning a new Museum of Mississippi History since the mid-1990s, but the project had not received funding. Efforts to establish a civil rights museum had been under way for years, culminating in a 2007 proposal to build a Mississippi Civil Rights Museum at Tougaloo College, but funding issues also stalled its success.

However, beginning in 2010, we worked with former governor William F. Winter and legislative leaders to build support for the idea of joining the two museums under the Department of Archives and History, and supporters of each museum united behind this new vision. In 2011 the Mississippi Legislature provided bond funds for planning and initial construction. Over the next five years, the legislature provided additional bond funds, eventually totaling $90 million. The commitment of our elected officials to the 2 Mississippi Museums is strong and unwavering, and we are grateful for their support.

The private sector, too, has been extremely generous in supporting the 2 Mississippi Museums. Right from the start, corporations, individual donors, and foundations came on board with gifts that eventually totaled more than $17 million. We deeply appreciate their leadership and their generosity.

On October 24, 2013, we broke ground for the museums, joining Governor Phil Bryant, former governors Ronnie Musgrove and William F. Winter, Myrlie Evers and other civil rights leaders and dignitaries, teachers, children, and other friends on the shovel line. Hundreds of Mississippians from across the state traveled to Jackson to celebrate with us on that glorious fall day, and we all watched with great excitement as the buildings rose from the ground over the next few years.

Even before they were complete, the museums began to make a significant economic impact as a construction project. The Mississippi Development Authority estimates that the impact will total more than $17 million per year. The museums will be a tourism portal, drawing visitors into Mississippi and then sending them out across the state to the places where history happened.

Though the economic impact is important, education is at the core of the two museums' mission. The largest classrooms in the state, the museums will welcome thousands of schoolchildren each year. Teachers will learn new ways to bring history to life in their classrooms. Through distance learning opportunities, online resources, and traveling exhibits and programs, the museums will reach many more people than those who walk through the door.

The impact of these museums will be felt across Mississippi and well beyond our state. They will not only inform our understanding of the past but will illuminate our way forward together. The stories we tell in these two museums are not just Mississippi's stories but America's stories. We are proud to join with our many project partners in sharing these stories with you.

Introduction

MYRLIE EVERS AND WILLIAM F. WINTER

O N OUR 200th ANNIVERSARY of statehood, Mississippi made history, opening the Museum of Mississippi History and the Mississippi Civil Rights Museum side by side in downtown Jackson. Mississippi's is the first state-operated civil rights museum in the nation.

It has been a great privilege for each of us to be a part of the campaign to build the 2 Mississippi Museums. And it is with tremendous satisfaction that we join with friends from across the state to celebrate their completion.

These museums are critical to the educational and cultural life of our state. No state has more stories to tell than we do. Stories of the native people who were here first, of Europeans and Africans, and later, immigrants from many lands—China, Italy, Vietnam, Greece, Lebanon, India, Mexico, and dozens more. Stories, too, of writers, artists, musicians, and craftspeople. Our history is not one narrative but all of these stories woven together. Fascinating and complex, tragic and inspiring, all of these stories have found a place in these two museums.

Fountain pen, plastic and metal, made by Shaffer's, ca. 1963. This fountain pen was recovered from the office desk of Medgar Evers after his assassination. The NAACP leader penned numerous letters over his career, initiating and supporting civil rights efforts across the country. His work helped focus national attention upon the intense social and political issues plaguing the state, raising the profile of Mississippi's Civil Rights Movement.

We have witnessed the progress our state has achieved since the dismantling of the "closed society." These museums capture that journey along with earlier struggles as Mississippi formed a state, fought a war, rebuilt an economy, and created a rich culture that still exists today. These stories and memories—told through the voices of the people who lived them—come alive here in these two museums. It is our hope that they will inspire us to work together to build a more just, vibrant, and healthy Mississippi for our future.

What is so important, and such a profound cause for celebration, is that we have built these museums together—side by side. When buses pull up loaded with schoolchildren, they pull up to one site. People from all across Mississippi will come in using one entrance. They will go through both museums together. This will be more than an educational institution—it will be a place of inspiration. We took different roads here, but we have built something new together—2 Mississippi Museums. We both plan to be frequent visitors. Join us.

MUSEUM OF MISSISSIPPI HISTORY

Introduction

DENNIS J. MITCHELL, PHD

ALL MISSISSIPPIANS deserve a place where our memories can be preserved, where our stories can be shared, and where our history can inspire and teach us. Our state now has such a place: the Museum of Mississippi History. This new museum will not only exhibit artifacts, images, and documents, but will knit them together through our voices, telling our stories for the generations of Mississippians who will follow us.

The Mississippi Department of Archives and History has been collecting our state's history since 1902. The construction of this new building allows MDAH to present the collection to the public in new and exciting ways. The Museum of Mississippi History will cover the entire sweep of the state's history, from earliest times to the present, with the benefit of the newest interactive technology and exhibit design.

That history will be told as never before—a story of violence and human conflict but also of endurance, inspiration, and a fierce sense of place. Visitors will learn about Native Americans' lives and the exploration and eventual settlement by Africans and Europeans bound together by the brutality of slavery as men and women were imported to Mississippi from Africa, the Caribbean, and the older eastern states.

Visitors to the Museum will learn about secession, the Civil War, Reconstruction, changing constitutions, the great migration, floods, two world wars, the impact of technology on farming, the diversification and industrialization of the economy, civil and voting rights gained by women and blacks, the development of public education, and the creation of some of the world's best music, literature, and art.

The narrative presented in this museum and book is the beneficiary of years of research by scholars from all fields of study. That narrative is enriched

Desk, wood and iron, early twentieth century. This desk was once used at Mississippi University for Women, which was the first public women's college in the United States. Then known as the Industrial Institute and College, the institution was created by an act of the Mississippi Legislature on March 12, 1884, for the dual purposes of providing a liberal arts education for women and preparing them for employment.

by journals, family heirlooms, and other treasures donated by thousands of Mississippians over the years. Visitors will encounter more than 1,500 of these artifacts as they travel back in time—from the flag that flew over the United States in 1818 to a boll weevil trap, rare quilts, military weapons and uniforms, letters, and even a clock that stopped at the moment Hurricane Katrina hit the house.

This museum will play an important role in sharing our stories, clearing away myths, and inspiring our children and grandchildren. The opening of this museum, side by side with the Mississippi Civil Rights Museum, sends a clear signal about the progress made in our state. By allowing us to understand fully who we are and where we came from, the 2 Mississippi Museums will help us make Mississippi a better place.

The First Peoples

EVERYTHING WE know about Mississippi's prehistory (before written records, or prior to 1519) comes from archaeological evidence, which reveals a cultural evolution from the Paleo-Indian Period to the Mississippian Period.

When the last Ice Age ended more than 15,000 years ago, Mississippi looked much different from how it does today. The first people who migrated to this area walked across the Mississippi River, then a shallow, braided stream surface. These Native Americans adopted a hunter-gatherer lifestyle, hunting small game, fishing, and gathering wild food.

Ongoing discoveries in the state paint a picture of the complex, skilled, and innovative people who flourished here. From stunning stone beads uncovered in the Keenan Cache to the sophisticated social complexes studied today at places like Emerald Mound, evidence from Mississippi shapes archaeologists' understanding of prehistoric life.

13,000–8000 BC	PALEO-INDIAN PERIOD Ice Age ends and people hunt white-tailed deer, black bear, and turkey.
8000–500 BC	ARCHAIC PERIOD hunting and gathering practices emerge and regional trade networks develop.
500 BC–AD 1000	WOODLAND PERIOD corn is introduced and bow and arrow invented.
AD 1000–1550	MISSISSIPPIAN PERIOD chiefdoms emerge and large temple mounds develop as ceremonial sites.

Prehistoric Tools

Much of what we know about Mississippi's prehistory comes from studying stone artifacts, since tools made of wood or other organic substances disappear over time. Skilled craftsmen created these stone tools for hunting, preparing food, and making clothing. In the Paleo-Indian Period, Native Americans used hard stones to chip away flakes from brittle stones until they created a desired shape. The resulting tools included projectile points for hunting, scrapers for cleaning hides, celts for tilling land, and stoneware for grinding grains—types of tools that were used for thousands of years.

Vessel, steatite (soapstone), Archaic Period.
A cache of twelve vessels made from soapstone, which is not native to Mississippi,
was found at the Claiborne Site in Hancock
County. Archaeologists believe that the
vessels were trade items used by the Poverty
Point culture, which centered at the Jaketown
site near Belzoni, Mississippi.

NEW LAND, NEW LIFE

At the end of the Ice Age, melting water and heavy, coarse sediment from mile-thick northern glaciers flowed south to the Gulf of Mexico. Gradually, the water flow stabilized and carried fine sediment, transforming the Mississippi River from small streams into the powerful river we know today. Early Mississippians embraced the River and Delta regions, which provided fertile land, a constant water source, animals for food, and transportation routes. Contact with more distant regions fostered complex trade networks and provided access to new resources. Travel on the Mississippi River created a flow of goods and ideas between previously separated societies.

As people settled in more permanent locations during the Woodland Period, they began to cultivate crops, including gourds and sunflowers. Corn, beans, and squash provided a nutritionally complete diet. These crops, known as the "Three Sisters," act as co-cultivars—beans replace nitrogen that corn and squash remove from the soil, while the cornstalk provides a base for the bean plants to climb.

Hoe, Mill Creek chert, date unknown. This thirteen-inch-long hoe was made of non-local stone before European contact.

Celt, gray agate hafted in a reproduced wooden handle, Mississippian Period.

Chasse générale du chevreuil (Deer Hunt), illustration from Le Page du Pratz's *Histoire de la Louisiane,* v. 2, 1758. Drawings by Le Page du Pratz are some of the earliest depictions of the Native Americans who lived in the area that would become the state of Mississippi. This illustration shows a group of hunters with bows and arrows.

Prehistoric Mississippians developed tools such as the bow and arrow and the atlatl—used to launch a spear greater distances—to hunt black bears, white-tailed deer, and turkeys from up to 250 feet away. Hunters learned where these and other animals migrated, allowing them to establish seasonal hunting territories. Along the edges of coasts and rivers, fishermen used fishweirs (traps) and hooks carved from bone to catch fish.

INDIGENOUS INNOVATION

Over the course of Mississippi's vast prehistory (12,500 years, or around 480 generations), people developed sophisticated cultures and products. Native Americans honed their skills, creating intricate and meaningful objects, from Paleo-Indian projectile points to Mississippian pottery, effigy beads, and adornments. As early as the Middle Archaic Period, the inhabitants of Mississippi developed methods for moving tons of dirt to create ceremonial mounds.

The Evolution of Projectile Points

During the Paleo-Indian Period, Native Americans crafted spears by inserting projectile points into a notch on the end of a wooden shaft. Early Paleo-Indian projectiles included large, bifacial points that were created in a process known as flint-knapping wherein craftsmen used an antler tool to remove small flakes from each side of the stone to achieve a sharp, straight edge.

Points became more diverse in size and shape throughout the prehistoric periods, some with notched corners and sides, as well as flutes in the middle. Notched points provided a groove for securing the point to a stick, allowing hunters to more easily retrieve the points after a kill for repeated use. As Native Americans improved flaking techniques and created new weapons, projectile points became smaller and more intricate, allowing them to be launched at higher speeds and with greater accuracy.

Wolf Lake type projectile point, Dover chert, Late Archaic Period.

Herring Cache: projectile point, novaculite points, green slate banner stones, Middle Archaic Period. These objects washed out of the Sardis Lake Reservoir and were found together by Robert L. Herring Sr.

The Development of Pottery

More than 3,000 years ago, in the Late Archaic Period, Native Americans began creating simple ceramic vessels from clay mixed with other materials, which they fired over an open flame to increase durability. The pottery was strictly utilitarian and was often discarded after a single use.

To increase strength and reduce cracking during the firing process, materials like sand, crushed stone, shell, or plant fibers were added to the clay as tempering agents. Stronger vessels could withstand repeated use for food preparation or for storing food during long winter months.

Pottery rapidly evolved during the subsequent Woodland and Mississippian Periods, from simple, utilitarian bowls to elaborately decorated vessels that could include handles and/or spouts. Mississippian Period pottery became more diverse as techniques evolved and trading opened access to new materials. Native Americans created incised pottery by pressing sticks or bones into wet clay. People began using cord, fabrics, and stamps to make impressions in wet ceramics. Colored tempers, like galena, hematite, or graphite, produced polychrome (multicolored) vessels.

Shell-tempered vessel with handles and incised and punctated animal designs, ceramic, Mississippian Period.

Shell-tempered Pouncey Ridge pinched jar with handles, ceramic, Late Mississippian Period.

Beads and Cultural Sophistication

For many years, archaeologists did not believe that people in the Middle Archaic Period possessed the time or technology to create intricate works of art. However, the discovery of the Keenan Cache in 1878 in Lawrence County unearthed 449 beads that proved otherwise. The beads, mostly red jasper, represent various stages of production, offering insight into the work of prehistoric craftsmen. Innovative craftsmen used the bow drill, which bored holes in long, narrow stones with great accuracy.

Native Americans traded with neighboring tribes for stone to make highly polished animal-shaped beads. These zoomorphic beads are thought to represent a strong religious belief system. Native Americans also traveled north along the Mississippi River, as far as current-day Ohio and Illinois, to trade for materials like high-quality stone and shell. They used these materials to create intricately carved pendants, called gorgets, which were symbols of wealth during the Mississippian Period.

Jaeger Bead Collection, carved stone including trachyte, red jasper, and quartzite, Middle Archaic Period. This group of beads was found at the Denton Site in the Northern Yazoo Basin. Several of the beads are zoomorphic, their shapes inspired by a variety of birds and mammals.

Building Mounds

People began moving tons of dirt to build mounds as early as the Middle Archaic Period, at first using them for burials. Later platform mounds included wooden ceremonial structures that honored high-ranking people, demonstrating a new hierarchy within tribes. Over time, builders created complexes, some consisting of more than ten mounds and covering acres of land where thousands of people lived.

Mississippi mounds are among the earliest known to exist in the United States; some are more than 7,000 years old. From Bear Creek Mound north of Tupelo to the Grand Village of the Natchez Indians to Graveline Mound on the Gulf Coast, mound sites across the state mark the centers of Native American societies. Emerald Mound, which served as a ceremonial center in the Mississippian Period, is Mississippi's largest ceremonial mound and the United States' second largest (after Monks Mound in Cahokia, Illinois). The site consists of multiple mounds, several of which are layered atop manmade plateaus. The ancestors of the Natchez Indians built Emerald Mound by using digging sticks and cane baskets to move more than six million cubic feet of dirt.

STORYTELLING

One way Choctaw and Chickasaw nations preserve their heritage is by passing down tales of prehistoric Mississippi through generations. Origin stories describe the creation of the earth and how each Tribe settled in Mississippi. Here are four stories recounted by the Tribes.

The Migration of the Chickasaw and Choctaw People

Guided by a sacred pole, two leaders named Chiksa' and Chahta led a group from the west. At the end of the day, they would stick the sacred pole straight into the ground, and each morning they traveled in the direction it was leaning.

One morning, Chahta was convinced that the upright pole signified that they had reached their homeland. Chiksa' disagreed, and believed that their homeland lay further eastward. The leaders parted ways, and the people who remained with Chiksa', still guided by the sacred pole, continued eastward to a place near present-day Pontotoc and Tupelo, Mississippi. There the pole stood straight, and the Chickasaw Nation knew they had found their homeland.

Nanih Waiya

In the Choctaw creation story, the Creator fashioned the first people from clay in an underground cave, known as Nanih Waiya Cave. The people crawled out from the earth to see the first light of day and lay upon the hillside until the clay dried. The first group to leave traveled east, and they are called the Muscogee. The next group went east as well, and they are called the Cherokee. The third group traveled north, and they are called the Chickasaw. The last group settled near the cave and built a mound known as Nanih Waiya. We call ourselves the Choctaw.

Story of the Squirrel Stick

A young, idle man fell in love with the *minko*'s daughter, but the disapproving leader refused to let him court her. Distraught, the young man knew he must change to impress the *minko'*.

One day, while whittling a stick, the young man came across a squirrel in the woods. He threw his stick at the squirrel, killing it. He returned each day, killing squirrels with his powerful stick, until the *minko'* took notice.

The young man impressed the village with his skill and successfully courted the *minko*'s daughter. The secret to his success remained hidden until his dying day, when he revealed the stick to his eldest son.

For generations, Chickasaw elders passed the secret of the Squirrel Stick to their eldest son, keeping the story alive today.

Tale of Mastodon Extinction

The Black Belt Prairie along the Tombigbee River was once a wooded forest heavily populated by large, elephant-like beasts. These mighty creatures roamed the land, eating leaves from the trees and gnawing at the bark, leaving behind the dead husks of a once lush forest.

The beasts roamed the land in bands, fighting each other. As time went on, the beasts fought until only two creatures remained. For many years, these mastodons walked the land until finally, they confronted each other. After a long battle, only one remained.

The surviving beast strode the land until it died in the prairie that we now call the Black Belt. This story is important to the Choctaw people because it demonstrates how long we have been living in our homelands.

ENDURING CULTURES

Mississippi's Native Nations created distinctive cultures and traditions, and this rich heritage remains strong and vibrant today. Eight present-day Native American Nations have historical roots in Mississippi: Alabama-Coushatta Tribe of Texas, The Chickasaw Nation, Choctaw Nation of Oklahoma, Jena Band of Choctaw Indians, Mississippi Band of Choctaw Indians, Muscogee Creek Nation, Quapaw Tribe of Indians, and Tunica-Biloxi Indian Tribe of Louisiana. In the early 1800s, forced land cessions and federal policy resulted in the removal of many native people to other places. Only the Mississippi Band of Choctaw Indians remains in the state, but the eight Tribes with Mississippi ties return here often to share and preserve their traditions.

Today, modern artisans use ancient techniques and natural materials to create traditional crafts. These objects are another way that traditions are preserved and passed down through generations.

"We have a time of tremendous growth and even greater potential ahead of us. As I said, the best is yet to come. Chikasha Poya. We are Chickasaw. We are blessed."
—GOVERNOR BILL ANOATUBBY, THE CHICKASAW NATION, 2015

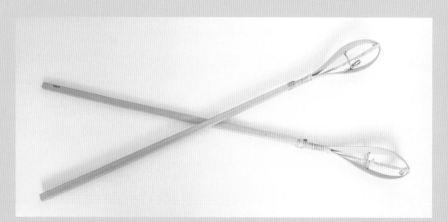

Stickball sticks, willow and buckskin, by Percy Pierrite, ca. 1962. Southeastern Tribes play a sport called stickball. Players each use a pair of sticks with pockets to throw and catch a cloth or leather ball, and points are scored at the team's own goalpost. The earliest written account of a game dates to 1700. Traditionally men and women played on teams that were usually from different villages. Native people followed rituals before and after games, such as song, dance, and purification. These stickball sticks follow the style of the Tunica Tribe.

"Our forefathers progressed and prospered because of their perseverance and resiliency. The Tribe continues to progress and prosper today because of that legacy."
—CHIEF GARY BATTON, CHOCTAW NATION OF OKLAHOMA, 2014

Cooking pot, clay and burned mussel shell, by Ian Thompson, ca. 2014. This cooking pot, or "Chahta Shutushi," is a miniature version of vessels made by Choctaw people 800 years ago. The clay was dug by hand in Alabama and mixed with burned mussel shell—or "tempered" to strengthen it. The maker shaped the pot by hand and fired it in an open wood fire.

Basket, river cane, by unknown Choctaw maker, early twentieth century. Choctaw artists have woven swamp cane into intricate, colorful baskets for centuries. Choctaw women harvest cane from riverbanks, then cut the stalks into strips, which were originally dyed using berries or other natural materials. Today, most basket makers use commercial dyes. The maker then weaves the strips together—this basket features a diamond pattern. In the 1940s or 1950s, this basket was purchased in Sandersville from a local Choctaw woman.

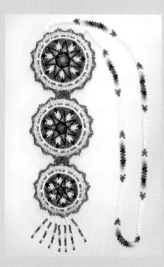

"We are experiencing a refreshing new day, a new beginning at Choctaw that is radiant with hope, promise, encouragement, inclusiveness, and most importantly, Choctaw Unity, which is a very positive source of our strength as Choctaw people."

—CHIEF PHYLISS J. ANDERSON, MISSISSIPPI BAND OF CHOCTAW INDIANS, 2016

Shirt, cotton, by unknown Chickasaw maker, 2014. In the 1700s and 1800s, European traders introduced new fabrics and materials to Mississippi. Native people began using them to make clothing, combining European styles with their own. The Chickasaw people added colored ribbons to cloth shirts, and the ribbons often represented family or clan colors.

Child's dress with apron, cotton or cotton blend, by Willie B. Willis, ca. 1970. Choctaw people adopted the clothing styles of early white settlers but maintained Choctaw characteristics such as vivid colors and triangle or diamond trim. Diamonds symbolize the unity of the Choctaw people. Today, traditional clothing is worn on ceremonial occasions.

Beaded necklace, glass backed with vinyl, by unknown Choctaw maker, ca. 2014. This intricate necklace features three beaded medallions in a traditional design. Early Choctaw makers used beads made from shells and dried seeds or berries. European traders introduced glass beads, which were more durable. Choctaw men and women wear beaded belts, collar necklaces, and sashes as part of ceremonial dress.

Cultural Crossroads

NATIVE AMERICANS, EUROPEANS, AND AFRICANS (1519–1798)

From 1519 to 1798, waves of European explorers, traders, and colonists came to Mississippi. Africans—most enslaved, some free—also arrived in this region. Native Americans had already developed sophisticated mound centers across Mississippi, but the region was more dramatically transformed as towns and fortifications developed at Ocean Springs, New Orleans, Mobile, Natchez, and other sites. Mississippians traded crops like tobacco, indigo, and cotton, as well as deerskin, with different partners as various colonial powers took control of the region. New commerce crisscrossed the territory, often following prehistoric trails like the Natchez Trace.

Spaniards first arrived in 1519 in southeastern North America, seeking gold and silver. Hernando de Soto and his conquistadors killed thousands of Native Americans at Mabila (in present-day Alabama) in October 1540. Mississippi's Native Americans fiercely resisted the hostile Spanish explorers, and De Soto never controlled this region. He died of a fever along the banks of a tributary west of the Mississippi River in 1542. By 1543, Native Americans forced the conquistadors to flee.

French explorers willing to coexist with Native Americans reached Mississippi in the late 1600s. They built the region's earliest European settlements and imported Mississippi's first enslaved Africans. Fearing British efforts to control the Mississippi River, French settlers constructed Fort Maurepas in 1699, the first permanent European community in Mississippi, near present-day Ocean Springs.

After a brief period of British control from 1763 to 1779, the Spanish regained power until signing a treaty yielding Mississippi to the United States by 1798. When the United States took over, the region's Native American population had begun to rebound from disease and conflict, but American

1519	Alonzo Alvarez de Piñeda reaches the mouth of the Mississippi River.
1540	Hernando de Soto begins his exploration of the Alabama-Mississippi region.
1682	Rene-Robert Cavelier, Sieur de La Salle, claims entire Mississippi Valley for France.
1699	Pierre Le Moyne, Sieur d'Iberville, establishes first European settlement in Mississippi.
1763	France transfers its lands east of the Mississippi River to England.
1779	Spanish occupy Natchez and assume control of Mississippi.
1798	Spain cedes Mississippi to the United States of America.

Muzzle-loading wheellock pistol, wood and steel, ca. 1650–1680. Firing mechanisms varied on firearms of this period. The wheellock, developed in the early sixteenth century, used a spinning wheel that showered sparks into a pan that held powder. The flintlock, created in the seventeenth century, sparked the powder using a trigger mechanism to release a flint that struck a steel plate.

expansion in the early 1800s threatened Native Americans' continued existence in Mississippi.

Tactical Advantages

Many believe that European explorers overcame Native American attacks because of their distinct advantage in weaponry, but the reality is more complex. Spanish explorers brought firearms to Mississippi, but they proved difficult to load and were often less effective than a Native American's bow and arrows, especially since Tribes were familiar with the terrain and capable of sophisticated guerrilla warfare.

Unlike the early Spanish explorers, French settlers traded guns to Mississippi's Native Americans as they colonized the region, arming Tribes so they could hunt to supply the booming deerskin trade. Tribes also defended themselves against the Chickasaw, who captured other Native Americans, handing them over as slaves to the English in exchange for more weaponry.

WHO CONTROLS MISSISSIPPI?

Diverse languages rang out across Mississippi as English, French, Native American, and Spanish people sought control over the region. Africans—both free and enslaved—had little voice in this new society. As colonial settlements like Natchez and Biloxi emerged, the non-native population of Mississippi grew from a few hundred in the early 1700s to 8,850—including 3,489 enslaved and 182 free black residents—by 1800.

The French introduced enslaved Africans to the Mississippi area during their colonial rule over Louisiana (1682–1763). French landowners deployed enslaved people to plant tobacco and indigo, and slaves remained in the region throughout British and Spanish control. In 1685, France enacted the *Code Noir* (*Black Code*) to regulate the life, purchase, religion, treatment, and even death of enslaved people in French colonies. Slaveholders often ignored the laws, treating the enslaved as they pleased, and once the British assumed control in 1763, *Code Noir* no longer applied in Mississippi. Shortly after Mississippi became a United States territory in 1798, the introduction of the cotton gin made cotton profitable and increased demand for laborers. Importation of enslaved people—from Africa and other American regions—soared. By 1840, blacks outnumbered whites in Mississippi.

Shackles, hand-forged wrought iron, eighteenth century. Enslaved people performed a variety of skilled tasks, including blacksmithing and metalwork, creating kitchen tools, farming implements, and even restraints like these shackles.

Natchez, Mississippi's Vital Center

French colonists founded Natchez in 1716, creating one of the most important European settlements in the region. The town's location along the Mississippi River made it a hub for trade and cultural exchange. Native American, Spanish, French, British, and African cultures intermingled here—sometimes peacefully, sometimes violently.

French colonists built Fort Rosalie soon after founding Natchez in 1716. The British gained control over the region and renamed the site Fort Panmure in 1764. By 1797, the Spanish occupied Fort Panmure. The following

A new and general map of the southern dominions belonging to the United States of America (detail), map by Robert Laurie and James Whittle, 1794. This late eighteenth-century map shows the former southern boundary of the United States as it met the 31st parallel. President George Washington sent Andrew Ellicott to survey this parallel in 1797. He arrived in Natchez on February 24 and set up camp on a bluff. Today, that site is called Ellicott's Hill.

year, Mississippi joined the United States, and the Americans rechristened this structure Fort Sargent for Winthrop Sargent, the first governor of the Mississippi Territory.

A 1784 census of the Natchez district counted a population of 1,619, including 498 enslaved Africans. Many of the remaining 1,121 people were French, Spanish, or free Africans. British and American immigration increased so rapidly that the majority of the town's residents spoke English by 1787—even though Spain still controlled this area.

Strongholds of Safety

Forts were centers of settlement, trade, and protection. Fort St. Pierre (destroyed by the Natchez in 1729) was the main French colonial settlement and a key trading post in the Yazoo Basin of the Mississippi River. In the 1730s, Mississippi's French forts became hubs for trading with Native Americans. The Spanish also built bulwarks like Fort Nogales along the Yazoo River to ward off European and American enemies. Meanwhile, Native Americans constructed their own defensive fortifications.

MISSISSIPPI IN TRANSITION

European concepts of inheritance, religion, and money challenged ancient cultural practices of Mississippi's native people. Many Native Americans lived in matrilineal societies in which the female line determined descent

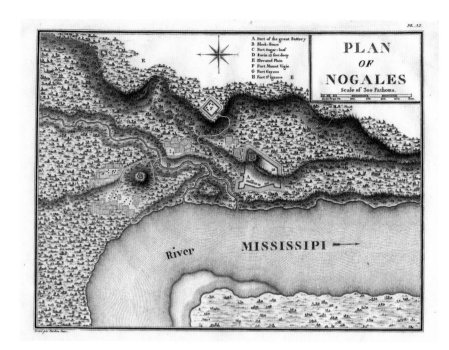

Plan of Nogales, map by Jean Baptiste Pierre Tardieu, 1797. From Victor Collot's *Voyage dans l'Amerique Septentrionale*, 1826.

Beads, glass, ca. 1492–1560; **Bell,** brass, seventeenth or eighteenth century; **two reales** (coin from Spain), silver, 1783; **Duit** (coin from Dutch East Indies), copper, 1754. Between 1519 and 1798, many European currencies flowed through Mississippi. By 1600 the British, French, and Dutch used manillas, or copper bracelets once used as currency in Africa, to buy enslaved people. Hernando de Soto and his men brought along glass beads from Italy, brass bells, and other small metal tools to present as gifts to the people they met. The French also traded with crafted items, such as brass bells, as well as more traditional forms of money. French, Spanish, British, and Dutch merchants all used coins in Mississippi. After the United States of America declared independence, continental currency in the form of paper bills circulated around the region.

and relationships, while French and Spanish laws and traditions favored the male, or paternal, line. Though many Native Americans ultimately adopted Christianity, they continued certain spiritual practices, like smoking from a calumet (ceremonial pipe). Trade patterns were also influenced by the arrival of Europeans. Mississippi's Native Americans had traded with societies as far away as modern Mexico, Central America, and Canada, but European contact introduced Mississippi to the transatlantic trade. Goods and people—including enslaved Africans—arrived from Europe and Africa at ports like Natchez and New Orleans. Monetary systems and currencies shifted with each ruling European power.

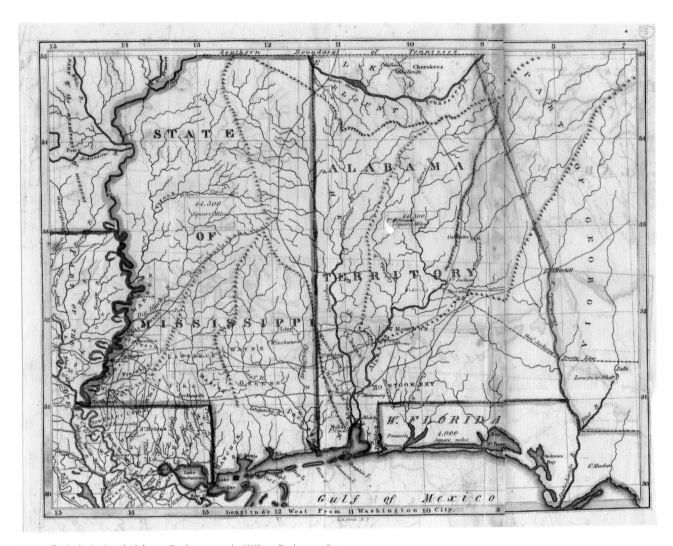

State of Mississippi and Alabama Territory, map by William Darby, ca. 1817.

Joining the United States

MISSISSIPPI FEVER" was driven by a mad dash for fertile land to grow cotton. White settlers poured into the Mississippi Territory. Organized in 1798, it encompassed much of present-day Mississippi and Alabama. The population swelled from 8,850 in 1800 to 136,621 in 1830. Nearly half of the new Mississippians were enslaved. White leaders forced the Choctaw and Chickasaw Tribes to give up more than thirty million acres of their Mississippi homelands.

Two wars and countless smaller disputes over land pitted American settlers against Native Americans, the Spanish, British forces, and one another. Despite disagreements between wealthy planters along the Mississippi River and small farmers in the eastern parts of the territory, Mississippi passed a constitution in 1817 and became a state. In the 1830s, the eviction of Native Americans led to an economic explosion based on slave-produced cotton, and by 1833, Mississippi was the third largest cotton producer in the United States.

1798	Congress establishes Mississippi Territory.
1812	War of 1812 commences; armed conflict lasts until February 1815.
1813–1814	Creek Indian War
1817	Mississippi becomes the twentieth state.
1830	President Andrew Jackson signs Indian Removal Act; Choctaws cede all remaining land in Mississippi.
1832	Chickasaws agree to the Treaty of Pontotoc, ceding lands east of the Mississippi River.

OPENING THE TERRITORY

In May 1798, American surveyor Andrew Ellicott began to mark the border between the Mississippi Territory and Spanish colonial holdings along the 31st parallel. The territory's original boundaries were the Mississippi and Chattahoochee Rivers in the west and east, the 31st parallel in the south, and the point where the Yazoo River empties into the Mississippi River in the north. To pay off debts to merchants and traders, the Choctaw made their first large land cession in 1805, adding much of today's southern Mississippi to the existing triangle that was the Natchez District. In 1810 the United States annexed Spanish "West Florida" along the Gulf Coast, and the eastern section joined the territory in 1812. By 1813, the Mississippi Territory encompassed present-day Alabama and Mississippi. On March 3, 1817, Congress divided the Mississippi Territory—within the year, the western section would become the state of Mississippi, and the eastern section the Alabama Territory, the same boundary used between the states today.

Forced Removal

The Choctaw and Chickasaw Tribes still occupied two-thirds of Mississippi in 1820, but by 1830, white and enslaved settlers outnumbered Native Americans by more than four to one. Pressured by US treaty negotiators, internal divisions, and crop failures, most of Mississippi's native people forfeited land. In a series of treaties, the Choctaws ceded nearly 24 million acres of land to the United States between 1800 and 1830.

In 1829 Mississippi claimed jurisdiction over Choctaw and Chickasaw lands within its borders. The following year, the federal government approved the Indian Removal Act. Hoping to retain their land, some Choctaw chiefs adopted Western concepts of land ownership, Christianity, and schooling. The 1830 Treaty of Dancing Rabbit Creek forced nearly 18,000 Choctaws to exchange communal land holdings for small individual plots or leave. The first of three waves of Choctaw—some 6,000 people—left Mississippi in October 1831. By 1834 all but 5,000 of Mississippi's Choctaws accepted forced removal to Oklahoma. The Chickasaws left no people in Mississippi because all were forced to move.

THE STATE OF MISSISSIPPI

Divisive politics, as well as the Creek War and the War of 1812, slowed progress to statehood as political factions vied for power. In 1817 President James Madison agreed to admit the western section of the territory as a state and organize the eastern section as the Alabama Territory. Delegates drafted a

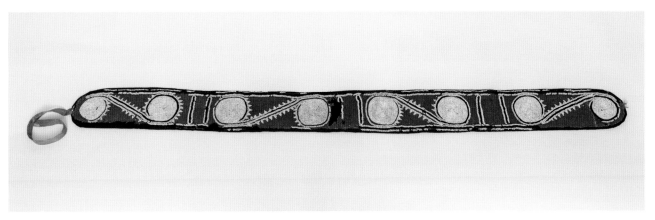

Baldric, fabric with glass beads, by unknown Chickasaw maker, ca. 1830. Chickasaw leader William Colbert presented this beaded sash as a gift to Dr. John H. Miller. Colbert died in 1836, a year before Chickasaw removal began.

constitution that sealed statehood on December 10, 1817. Mississippi's wealthy plantation owners and small farmers disagreed on voting rights and how to govern new lands taken from Native Americans, leading to two constitutional conventions—in 1817 and 1832. African Americans and Native Americans had no voice in creating or governing Mississippi.

Fighting Two Wars

Spain controlled land along the Gulf of Mexico until 1812 and allowed illegal British trade with the Creek Tribe. Tensions rose because the United States feared an alliance of the Europeans with the Creeks. Mississippi militia fought in the Creek War (1813–1814), which became entwined with the larger American conflict with Britain, the War of 1812 (1812–1815).

The Creek Nation divided over American encroachment on its lands in the eastern Mississippi Territory, present-day Alabama. Seeking to protect their society, "Red Stick" Creeks began attacking white settlers and Creeks who supported friendship with the United States. In the summer of 1813, a group of Mississippi militia, including pioneer and soldier Samuel Dale, ambushed Creeks at Burnt Corn Creek. Creek forces then attacked Fort Mims, near Mobile, killing hundreds of settlers and pro-white Creeks. The Mississippi militia joined US forces and Native American allies to defeat the Red Stick Creeks at Horseshoe Bend in March 1814.

Double-breasted uniform coat, hand-woven, indigo-dyed blue wool with Sheffield silver buttons, ca. 1809–1811. Members of the territorial militia included men like Andrew Marschalk, "the Father of Mississippi Journalism," who had moved from New York to Natchez in the 1790s, bringing a printing press and publishing several early newspapers. This coat was worn by Marschalk, who served as a major and colonel in the militia.

The United States declared war on Great Britain in June 1812. In early 1813, fearing an invasion by British forces, over 600 Mississippi militia marched from Washington, Mississippi, to Baton Rouge "as Americans united to maintain the best interests of their country." During the war, more than 1,600 men joined territorial militia units like the 1st Mississippi Infantry, the Mississippi Dragoons, and the Natchez Volunteer Riflemen. Fighting alongside other American troops in Pensacola and Mobile and at the Battle of New Orleans, these men helped secure the US victory in 1815, ending Spanish and British claims in the Mississippi Territory and devastating the Creeks.

Set of rifled percussion-cap dueling pistols, silver, gold leaf, mahogany, and ebony, early to mid-nineteenth century. Once owned by Seargent S. Prentiss, these pistols are ornately carved and engraved, and feature a silver shield with engraved family crest inset into the wood of each weapon.

Bowie knife and silver sheath, steel with ebony grip and silver fittings, made by Henry Schively, 1831. Rezin Bowie presented this early copy of the Bowie knife to Jackson resident Jesse Perkins.

The Custom of the Duel

Elite white men dueled with one another using special pistols or swords, and received legal immunity for their actions, a privilege not shared by other Mississippians. Some participants in the duel followed an international set of twenty-six rules called the *code duello*, which regulated everything from the contest's time of day to the extent of injuries required to satisfy participants' "honor." This custom continued until the 1832 Constitution authorized the legislature to outlaw dueling.

Mississippi congressmen, Supreme Court justices, and at least three governors engaged in duels over personal and political conflicts. Future governor George Poindexter mortally wounded Abijah Hunt in one infamous 1811 duel. Vicksburg lawyer Seargent S. Prentiss dueled three times with future governor Henry S. Foote over a courtroom skirmish, the series ending when Prentiss wounded Foote.

After an 1827 duel on a sandbar above Natchez ended with a handshake, a melee broke out among spectators. Famed frontiersman Jim Bowie was badly wounded in the fight, but he managed to kill his sword-wielding opponent with a large knife. Bowie's brother Rezin P. Bowie took credit for designing the now-famous Bowie knife.

Move for Statehood

Federal law required a territorial population of 5,000 before citizens could choose their own leaders. Small farmers believed that the federally appointed governor, Massachusetts native Winthrop Sargent, governed arbitrarily, and they complained to Congress, which established a territorial legislature before Mississippi met the population threshold. After the 1814 Treaty of Fort Jackson opened Creek lands in the eastern section of the Mississippi Territory to white settlement, its population increased. Mississippi's territorial delegate to Congress, William Lattimore, introduced a bill to divide the territory in two, paving the way for Mississippi statehood and carving out Alabama as a separate territory.

In March 1817 Congress approved admitting the western section of the Mississippi Territory as a state and called for a constitutional convention. In August, forty-seven delegates—70 percent of them from the Natchez district—signed a constitution favoring affluent planters. President James Monroe accepted the constitution, and Mississippi became the twentieth state on December 10, 1817.

Mississippi voters elected David Holmes as the first governor of the new state. He had previously served as territorial governor, appointed to the position in 1809 by Thomas Jefferson. He was succeeded by George Poindexter in 1820, who pushed for a Revised Code of the Laws of Mississippi, the first codification of the state's laws.

As Mississippi added land and settlers, voters approved a referendum on a new constitutional convention by a four-to-one margin. The 1832 Constitution reflected a national movement to expand suffrage by allowing all free white males over age twenty-one to vote. The document also eliminated property qualifications for candidates, and put almost every state and county office on the ballot. Mississippi became the first state to elect all of its judges.

Territorial seal of Mississippi embosser, cast bronze, 1798. This seal, which features an incorrect spelling of the territory's name, was cast in Philadelphia, Pennsylvania, then the nation's capital. Daniel Tilton, one of the Mississippi Territory's first judges, brought it with him after his May 1798 commissioning.

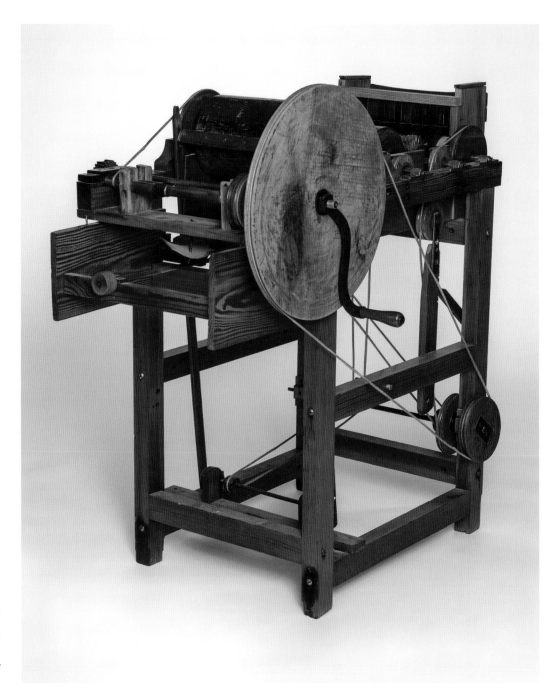

Cotton gin, wood, metal, and leather, ca. 1840. The invention of the cotton gin in the late eighteenth century revolutionized the cotton industry, with early machines cleaning cotton fifty times faster than a person could.

SLAVERY AND COTTON

The discovery that cotton thrived in Mississippi created an economic opportunity for settlers who had already tried tobacco and indigo as their cash crops. Slave-owning planters realized fantastic profits by selling their crops to northern and European textile mills, and they became among the wealthiest people in the country. Cotton accounted for over half of US exports in the first half of the 1800s.

To satisfy the demand for land to plant cotton, the government auctioned off former Chickasaw and Choctaw territories. Some planters moved their entire plantation operations—including enslaved African Americans—to Mississippi. Planters viewed enslaved people as valuable "property." In 1830 a slave sold at about $900, or around 10,000 times the price of a pound of cotton. The forced migration of African Americans to the Deep South, which began in the early 1800s, is often called "the second middle passage."

Mississippi's cotton production soared from practically nothing in 1800 to 70 million pounds in 1833, increasing the demand for slave labor. Between 1800 and 1830, Mississippi's enslaved African American population grew from 3,489 to 65,659—almost 1.5 times the increase in the white population. By 1859, Mississippi produced more cotton than any other US state.

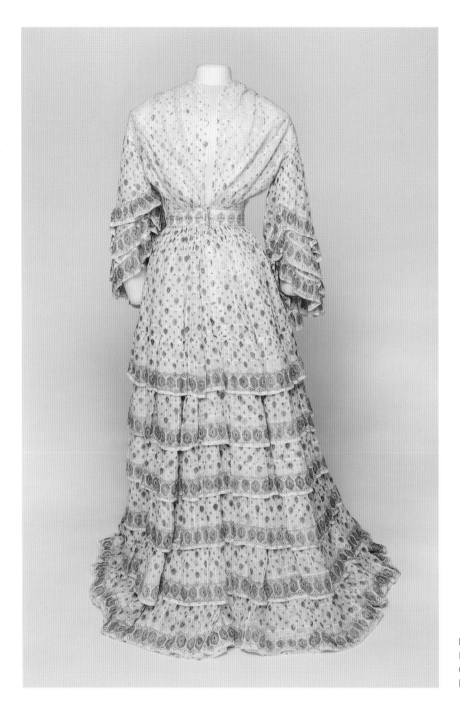

Day dress, cotton, 1856. Wealthy
Mississippians, including Addie Clark
Glover who owned this dress, wore the
latest fashions.

Cotton Kingdom

ENSLAVEMENT AND CIVIL WAR
(1833–1865)

As the 1830s drew to a close, Mississippians populated lands taken from the Choctaw and Chickasaw. Plantations spread east from the Mississippi River. Cotton exports created great wealth for cotton planters, who depended on enslaved African Americans to cultivate the cash crop. African Americans outnumbered whites in the state by 1840.

After the Mexican-American War, white Mississippians participated in a national debate, arguing that territories gained from the conflict should become slave states. In 1861, the majority of Mississippi's leaders asserted that preserving slavery meant leaving the United States. Most white Mississippians believed any conflict between North and South would not last long. Instead, the Civil War lasted four years and left hundreds of thousands dead, maimed, widowed, and orphaned. Fighting in the state destroyed the cotton kingdom. Black Mississippians rejoiced because the war gave them freedom, but they faced white retaliation.

1837	Economic panic threatens economy.
1846	Jefferson Davis leads 1st Mississippi Infantry in the Mexican-American War.
1859	Mississippi becomes leading cotton producer in America.
1861	Mississippi secedes from the United States and the Civil War begins.
1863	Emancipation Proclamation declares "all persons held as slaves" in Confederate states to be free.
1865	Confederate army surrenders, ending the Civil War.

EXPANDING AND DIVERSIFYING AGRICULTURE

When cotton prices dropped by 25 percent during an 1837 economic depression, Mississippi's farmers had to make improvements to existing crops and systems or diversify their crops in order to survive. Agricultural production expanded, and planters relied on the Mississippi River more than ever to import slaves and export goods. Henry W. Vick developed improved cotton strains at Nitta Yuma, his Deer Creek plantation, in the 1840s. Vick's cotton bolls opened wider and could be picked more easily, enabling field workers to

Steamer *Charles D. Shaw* docked at riverbank in Natchez, photograph by Robert Livingston Stewart, ca. 1890. The Mississippi River served as the main transportation and shipping artery of the region, with nearly 1,000 steamships on its water at the start of the Civil War. This steamboat, the *Charles D. Shaw*, carried passengers and trade goods in and out of Natchez until 1896.

harvest 200 pounds each day—four times the yield of older varieties. Planters also grew sweet potatoes, corn, oats, barley, peanuts, and sorghum cane. In northern Mississippi, growers cultivated wheat, reducing dependence on the Midwest for grains. Planters developed strategies to replenish the soil by rotating crops and growing peas, as Native Americans had done. Successful breeding produced heartier animals and enabled some farms to harvest wool for the first time. Throughout these agricultural innovations, cotton remained king. In 1859 the state turned out 535.1 million pounds of cotton, making Mississippi the leading cotton producer in the nation.

Horn with carved mouthpiece, possibly from a steer, ca. 1857. Born into slavery in Tennessee, William B. Randolph blew this horn to wake his fellow enslaved African Americans at Andrew Jackson Donelson Jr.'s Bolivar County plantation. Horns signaled daily schedules on many plantations.

Woman holding baby, daguerreotype, ca. 1850–1860. Enslaved people did not just toil in the fields; many, including the woman in the background of this photograph, were domestic workers. The photographer composed this portrait so that the focal point was on the white child, and the woman's face is not shown.

A Kingdom Built by Slaves

Cotton fields required constant attention much of the year. Slaveholders depended on enslaved African Americans to thin plants, remove weeds, and pick bolls. To increase output, Mississippi planters imported 217,329 black slaves into the state between 1830 and 1860. These enslaved people came from other states, particularly Virginia, North Carolina, Maryland, and Kentucky. The number of native-born slaves increased as well. The Forks of the Road market at Natchez was Mississippi's most active slave-trading site. Substantial slave markets also existed at Aberdeen, Crystal Springs, Vicksburg, Woodville, and Jackson.

DIVIDING LINES

Mississippians played an active role in American expansion during the mid-1800s. Soon after Texans declared independence from Mexico in 1836, proslavery politicians from Mississippi and other states called for Texas to join the United States as a slave state. In 1845 the United States annexed Texas, setting off an armed conflict with Mexico. President Polk appointed Mississippi governor John A. Quitman one of six brigadier generals commanding US forces.

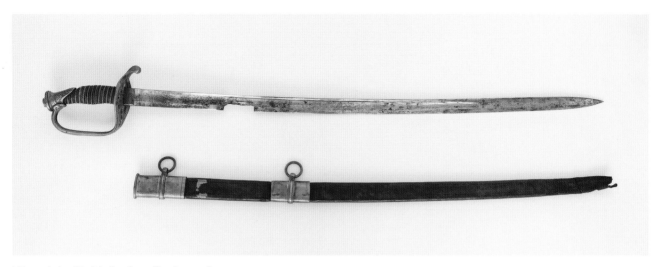

US regulation Model 1850 foot officer's sword and scabbard, metal, gilded brass, and wood grip covered with fish skin, manufactured by W. H. Horstmann and Sons, ca. 1843–1859. Colonel Jefferson Davis presented Private John S. Holt with this sword and scabbard for gallantry in the Mexican-American War.

When a call for Mississippi soldiers went out, more than 2,000 organized into companies and reported to Vicksburg to fight. A regiment of ten companies, each composed of 100 soldiers, elected Jefferson Davis of Warren County as their colonel. The 1st Mississippi Infantry, nicknamed the "Mississippi Rifles," advanced on Mexican soldiers during the Battle of Buena Vista, during which fewer than 5,000 US forces defeated 15,142 Mexican troops. After nearly two years of fighting, the Mexican-American War officially ended on February 2, 1848. America gained almost one million square miles of territory.

Arguments over slavery escalated after the Mexican-American War. Mississippi politicians participated in a national debate on the future of slavery in new states and territories. Abolitionist crusaders spoke out, and northern states refused to enforce the return of runaway slaves. Republican presidential candidate Abraham Lincoln opposed the extension of slavery into the territories, and many Mississippians believed that his 1860 victory would end slavery altogether. In the 1850s a group of politicians known as "fire-eaters" sought to persuade their constituents that secession was the only way to maintain slavery.

Mississippi governor John J. Pettus convened a special session of the state legislature on November 26, 1860, urging legislators to authorize the election of delegates to a secession convention. By an 84–15 vote, those delegates to

Quilt, "Honeycomb" or "Martha Washington's Flower Garden" pattern, cotton, made by Millies Lake, 1848. Enslaved African Americans produced items like this quilt, both for their owners and for slave households. Millies Lake was freed by her owners, William and Clementine Lake of Grenada.

Necklace, copper and garnets, mid-nineteenth century. This necklace was stolen from a Jackson home by Union soldier Daniel Jones of Company I, 17th Iowa Infantry. Jones wrote about the "plundering of Jackson" in a letter to his sister. His descendants returned the necklace, as well as the letter, to Mississippi in 2010.

the convention voted to secede on January 9, 1861. The Declaration of Secession stated, "Our position is thoroughly identified with the institution of slavery—the greatest material interest of the world." On January 23, the legislature organized the Army of Mississippi. The state joined the Confederacy in February 1861 and prepared to fight the United States.

A New President

A planter who owned more than 100 enslaved people, Jefferson Davis served as a Mississippi congressman, Mexican-American War colonel, and US secretary of war. As a US senator, Davis argued for the rights of slaveholding states, but he urged compromise instead of secession throughout the 1850s. Davis formally withdrew from the US Senate on January 21, 1861. The following month, the Confederate Congress elected Davis president. On February 18, 1861, he gave his first inaugural address as president of the Confederacy, asserting, "[W]e must prepare to meet the emergency and to maintain, by the final arbitrament of the sword, the position which we have assumed among the nations of the earth." On November 6, 1861, Davis won a full six-year term as president of the Confederacy.

THE CIVIL WAR

Almost 100,000 Mississippians served in the Civil War. Around 80,000 white Mississippians fought for the Confederacy. More than 17,000 black and 500 white Mississippians fought for the Union. Fighting occurred across the state and decimated cities like Jackson and Meridian. During the Meridian Campaign, Union general William T. Sherman's army destroyed railroads, locomotives, bridges, and other property in order to undermine the Confederate war effort. Throughout Mississippi, public buildings and private homes were converted into hospitals.

On the home front, white women managed farms and households while their husbands, sons, and brothers went to war. Unless they escaped to freedom or refused to work, enslaved people continued to labor in the fields or houses. As the conflict went on, however, some of the enslaved demonstrated their desire for freedom by fleeing to passing Union armies, especially after they received news of the Emancipation Proclamation.

Unimaginable Loss

During the Civil War, thousands of physicians were introduced to new standards of care, including the prevention and treatment of infectious disease, anesthetic agents, and surgical principles that advanced the quality of American medical practice. Despite these advances, three out of every ten Mississippi Confederate soldiers died in the Civil War. Battle wounds claimed the lives of about 12,000. An additional 15,000 Mississippi soldiers died from disease. Dysentery—caused by contaminated food or water—was the single greatest killer of Civil War soldiers.

In 1888 Mississippi began granting pensions to indigent Confederate veterans or their widows. Qualifying Mississippians received between twenty and thirty dollars each year. In 1900 Mississippi paid out $149,035 in Confederate pensions. The state also provided support to injured veterans. The number of Mississippi amputees was so staggering that the postwar government recommended spending some $200,000—20 percent of the state's budget—to purchase artificial limbs.

Remnants of Confederate flag, wool with silk in glass jar, ca. 1861–1865. This glass candy jar contains fragments of a Confederate flag carried by the 6th Mississippi Infantry during the Civil War. The person who preserved the remnants noted that seven color bearers were killed or wounded while carrying the banner during the April 1862 Battle of Shiloh, Tennessee.

A SENSE OF DUTY
Mississippians in the Military

Confederate soldier at Grenada, tintype, 1861. Tintypes were easier and less time-consuming to produce than daguerreotypes, thus allowing photographers to capture portraits of Civil War soldiers with greater ease in the field. Photographers used the wet collodion process to expose and develop images on thin, metal plates.

The tradition of military service runs deep in Mississippi. More than 20,000 men and women in Mississippi currently serve in the military on active duty or as civilian personnel. Another 17,000 are members of National Guard units or reserves in the US Armed Forces.

Mississippians have served throughout the state's history. Even before statehood, militia fought for the United States in the War of 1812. Mississippians—black and white—shed blood during the Civil War. Hundreds of thousands of Mississippians served in World Wars I and II. Men and women defended the United States in Korea, Vietnam, the global War on Terrorism, and more.

MAKING MISSISSIPPI
The American Revolution, 1775–1783; the War of 1812, 1812–1815; and the Creek War, 1813–1814

Three wars shaped Mississippi before statehood in 1817. During and after the American Revolution, British, American, and Spanish forces contested the Natchez District and command of the lower Mississippi River. In 1795 Spain acknowledged American control with Pinckney's Treaty, recognizing the 31st parallel as the southern boundary of the United States. When the United States went to war with Britain during the War of 1812, 1,667 Mississippi soldiers defended the young nation. At the same time, Mississippi militia and Choctaw warriors fought and defeated the "Red Stick" Creek Indians. The treaties signed after the Creek War and War of 1812 opened up Mississippi for continued American settlement.

"STAND FAST, MISSISSIPPIANS!"
The Mexican-American War, 1846–1848

Although President James K. Polk only requested 1,000 men from Mississippi, more than twice that number organized into companies and reported to Vicksburg. The volunteers were inspected, and ten companies from across the

Military uniform coat and sword belt,
wool and leather, ca. 1861–1865. T. Otis
Baker, a member of a wealthy merchant
family from Natchez, wore this coat and
sword belt in the Civil War. Baker enlisted
in the 10th Mississippi Infantry in 1862,
just six days before turning eighteen.
He fought at Shiloh, Murfreesboro,
Chickamauga, and other battles, eventually rising to the rank of captain.

Model 1841 percussion military rifle, wood, steel, brass, and iron, 1850 with alterations ca. 1857–1858. This muzzle-loading firearm is an example of a "Mississippi rifle."

Colt Model 1851 Navy revolver, wood, steel, and brass, manufactured by Colt Patent Firearms Manufacturing Company, patented 1850. Officers and cavalrymen favored revolvers because they could be fired rapidly without constant reloading. The six-shot Colt Model 1851 Navy revolver became the most popular sidearm in the Confederacy.

state were accepted to fight in the 1st Mississippi Infantry. Colonel Jefferson Davis led the forces during victorious battles at Monterrey and Buena Vista. Former congressman Davis used his influence to supply his soldiers with Whitney rifles, giving rise to the regiment's nickname, "the Mississippi Rifles." The Mississippi Rifles were designated the 155th Infantry Regiment in 1917 as part of the federalized National Guard.

FIGHTING A CIVIL WAR
The Civil War, 1861–1865

Mississippi seceded from the Union in 1861. Eighty thousand white Mississippians fought for the Confederacy. Some 17,000 African Americans from Mississippi fought for their own freedom in the Union Army as part of the US Colored Troops. Approximately 500 whites also fought for the Union. More than 300 engagements, large and small, were fought on Mississippi soil, across all parts of the state. The war took an incredible toll; as many as one-third of Mississippi's Confederate soldiers died. Others deserted or were permanently disabled in action.

Instruments of War

Early Civil War battles produced massive casualties because of improved weapons like the rifled musket and "minie" ball (fired from the barrel of a gun), more accurate artillery, and the numbers of troops engaged. While soldiers continued to use knives, swords, and bayonets, they accounted for less than 1 percent of weapons-related deaths. In July 1861 the Mississippi Legislature encouraged the Holly Springs firm McElwaine and Company to begin manufacturing rifles. The Confederate government soon ordered 30,000 Model 1841 Mississippi rifles from McElwaine. Although the British 1853 Enfield rifle was the most prevalent Confederate rifle, soldiers fought with over 100 different models of rifles, muskets, and carbines. Small arms fire contributed to some 90 percent of all battlefield casualties during the Civil War.

Burt Rifles flag, painted silk, by Lee Mallory, ca. 1861–1863. Mississippi's Confederate soldiers fought under flags representing command structures including companies, regiments, brigades, and armies. A group of Jackson women presented the men of Company K, 18th Mississippi Infantry, with this hand-painted flag. The Burt Rifles were named for Colonel Erasmus Burt, who died from wounds suffered at the Battle of Ball's Bluff, Virginia, in October 1861. He was the first Mississippi officer killed in a Civil War battle.

To counter the increased range of infantry weapons, armies relied on field fortifications, often using the natural advantages of the terrain to construct elaborate earthworks. During the siege of Vicksburg, and frequently throughout the rest of the war, both armies used extensive fortifications.

Artillery had played an important offensive role for centuries of armed conflict, but that changed during the Civil War. Commanders built breastworks (temporary fortifications) bristling with rifle-equipped infantry troops—artillery soldiers could not get close enough without coming under fire themselves. Thus, field artillery was often used in fixed positions to disrupt infantry formations or protect fortifications. At Vicksburg, Confederate defenders placed artillery on the bluffs and along the waterfront to guard the Mississippi River.

"REMEMBER THE MAINE"
The Spanish-American War, 1898

In the interest of extending American influence and gaining strategic ports in the Caribbean, the United States supported Cuba's 1890s struggle for independence from Spain. After the unexplained sinking of the USS *Maine* on February 15, 1898, America declared war on Spain. Mississippians sympathized with the Cuban cause and supported the war. Locals filled out the 1st, 2nd, and 3rd Mississippi Volunteer Infantry units. Mississippians also joined the 5th "Immunes," a US regiment composed of soldiers whom Congress believed would be immune to tropical diseases.

A STATE DIVIDED
World War I, 1914–1918

More than 57,000 Mississippians served during World War I. US Senator James K. Vardaman of Mississippi had cast one of only six votes against the declaration of war in 1917. Vardaman believed the fighting would fall mostly on poor people, like the farmers he represented. He also feared that allowing African Americans in combat would upend the racially segregated social order in Mississippi. At home, thousands worked to support the war effort, and the army

German Model 1916 Stahlhelm, painted steel, ca. 1916. This type of Stahlhelm (steel helmet) was the first modern combat helmet of the German army. The helmets were originally issued to soldiers painted in a gray-green color, but many units were allowed to camouflage them. This helmet's paint scheme is unusual because it incorporates pictures of women into the camouflage pattern.

Heart shield Bible, New Testament Bible with gold-plated steel cover, ca. 1944–1945. Families sent heart shield Bibles to protect soldiers during battle.

built Camp Shelby near Hattiesburg and Payne Field near West Point. Some 860 Mississippians died in World War I. In total, the war took over 18 million lives, of which 8.5 million were combat related.

WAR TRANSFORMS MISSISSIPPI
World War II, 1941–1945

After the Japanese bombed Hawaii's Pearl Harbor on December 7, 1941, Mississippians strongly supported the war effort. More than 237,000 Mississippians served in World War II—11 percent of the state's population. The federal government reactivated WWI-era Camp Shelby, which became the largest base in the state, followed by Keesler Air Field in Biloxi. Sixteen prisoner-of-war camps were established in the state. Private industries supporting the war effort—like Ingalls Shipbuilding—boomed. Thousands of Mississippians found employment. In some plants, women, many working in industry for the first time, composed 90 percent of the force.

THE COLD WAR HEATS UP
The Korean War, 1950–1953

During the Cold War, the United States and the Soviet Union divided most of the world into Communist and anti-Communist camps. After Communist North Korea invaded South Korea, nearly 75,000 Mississippians served with the US armed forces deployed to defend the south. Between 1951 and 1953, Mississippi lost 461 soldiers in the conflict. The Mississippi National Guard sent 6,515 individuals in support of United Nations–led peacekeeping operations. Four Mississippians were awarded the Congressional Medal of Honor. The Distinguished Flying Cross was awarded posthumously to Jesse L. Brown of Hattiesburg, who had become the first black naval aviator in 1948 and was killed in action in Korea in 1950.

CONFLICT AT HOME AND ABROAD
The Vietnam War, 1965–1975

Thousands of Mississippians served in the Vietnam War; 637 died in action. Milton L. Olive III, who had moved from Chicago to Lexington, and Roy M. Wheat of Moselle posthumously received the Medal of Honor. Most men were drafted into active-duty units, but in 1968 an entire army reserve unit from Greenwood was called up for service in Vietnam. At home, Mississippians built ships and trained personnel. The war proved controversial, further fueling debates on domestic problems.

WAR IN THE DESERT
The Gulf War, 1990–1991

The Gulf War, when Operation Desert Shield became Operation Desert Storm, began in 1990 when the United States led a coalition of nations to reverse Iraq's invasion of Kuwait. The military's Total Force Policy, which required all active and reserve military organizations to be treated as a single force, led to the activation of approximately 60,000 Army National Guard soldiers for the Gulf

War. Mississippi provided the largest National Guard contingent for the war effort. More than 6,500 Mississippi National Guard members, representing 70 units and 57 communities, served on active duty during the Gulf War.

ENDURING FREEDOM
War on Terrorism, 2001–

The 1990s saw a series of terrorist attacks against US forces in Saudi Arabia, Africa, and Yemen. After the coordinated terrorist attacks on September 11, 2001, in New York City, Pennsylvania, and Washington, DC, the United States launched a War on Terrorism. Mississippians have served in every campaign of the conflict, from the Middle East to the Philippines to Africa. The Mississippi National Guard mobilized more than 10,000 service members for multiple tours, with every deployable unit participating. After fighting ceased in Afghanistan, members of the Mississippi National Guard remained in Afghanistan to help local people rebuild and learn to produce sustainable farms.

OPERATION IRAQI FREEDOM
The Iraq War, 2003–2011

Mississippi National Guard units were among the first to enter the country as Operation Iraqi Freedom began in March 2003. American troops invaded Iraq in search of weapons of mass destruction, and Saddam Hussein was removed from power. Mississippi Guard members served a number of key roles during the war; for example, the 114th Army Liaison Team of Greenville assumed command of Abu Ghraib following incidents of prisoner abuse. Fifty-five Mississippians died during Operation Iraqi Freedom, which officially ended when US troops withdrew in 2011.

Military uniform coat, cotton and nylon with Universal Camouflage pattern, ca. 2009. Captain Darrell Baughn, US Army Reserve, served in Iraq in 2005 and Afghanistan in 2009 and 2010. He purchased this Universal Camouflage uniform in October 2009, when he deployed with the 412th Engineering Company out of Vicksburg.

Centerpiece, etched silver, manufactured
by J.E. Caldwell & Co., 1909. The people of
Mississippi commissioned silver pieces and
presented them to the second USS *Mississippi*
in Pascagoula on June 1, 1909. The centerpiece is etched with multiple scenes including
the Old Capitol, Hernando de Soto, Jefferson
Davis, an eagle, and magnolia and cotton
blossoms. The full silver service consists of
sixty-two pieces that were returned to the state
in 1956.

THE USS *MISSISSIPPI*

From 1841 to 1997, four different ships named USS *Mississippi* entered service, sailing in the Mexican-American War, the Civil War, World War II, the Vietnam War, and the Gulf War. In 2012 the navy commissioned the submarine USS *Mississippi*. The *Mississippis* and their sailors earned the name "Pride of the Fleet."

Officials commissioned the first USS *Mississippi* on December 22, 1841. This steam-powered vessel first saw combat in the Mexican-American War. In 1853 it served as Commodore Matthew Perry's flagship during his mission to Japan. During the Civil War, the vessel joined the Union naval squadron that captured New Orleans in April 1862. After it ran aground in the Mississippi River in March 1863, Union sailors set fire to the ship, destroying the *Mississippi* rather than risk its capture.

The second USS *Mississippi* (BB-23) was commissioned on February 1, 1908. In 1914 its crew assisted in constructing the nation's first naval aviation training center, Pensacola Naval Air Station. The ship participated in the US response to the Mexican Revolution in April 1914, and its naval aviators became the first to go into combat. Later that year, officials decommissioned the *Mississippi* and sold it to Greece. Its figurehead is displayed on the state capitol grounds.

A new, 32,000-ton USS *Mississippi* (BB-41) launched on January 25, 1917. The *Mississippi* earned eight battle stars in the Pacific during World War II. It served as flagship of a US battle line in the 1944 Battle of Leyte Gulf. The *Mississippi* anchored in Tokyo Bay for the Japanese surrender in 1945—the same place as the first USS *Mississippi* in 1853. After the war, the *Mississippi* tested experimental weapons, including the navy's first guided-missile system. The ship was decommissioned in 1956.

The nuclear-powered USS *Mississippi* (CGN-40), commissioned in 1978, was a guided-missile cruiser. It served during Operation Desert Shield in 1990 and Operation Desert Storm in 1991. The *Mississippi* was flagship of a multinational fleet on this extended deployment and launched Tomahawk cruise missiles into Iraq. In 1994 the ship helped enforce an embargo on Haiti. The *Mississippi* went on to coordinate air operations for humanitarian relief efforts in the war-torn former Yugoslavia in 1995. Two years later, naval officials decommissioned the ship.

"Reconciliation chair," wooden rocking chair painted by William Duffner, 1863. Indiana native Duffner served in the Union's 24th Indiana Volunteers and fought at the Battle of Port Gibson. The first shots were fired at the nearby home of A. K. Shaifer Jr., and the home served as a Union hospital. After the war, Shaifer befriended Union veterans who had fought on his property. Duffner made this illustrated chair depicting his regiment's movements at Port Gibson. The inscription reads, "From William Duffner, Yank. To Mr. A. K. Shaifer, Reb. in memory of May 1, 1863. The tack heads indicate my regiments line of march from dawn to dark. May God forgive unite and bless us all."

The World Remade

PASSED AND RATIFIED IN 1865, the Thirteenth Amendment to the US Constitution ended legalized slavery, dismantling a system that had defined Mississippi's economic, cultural, and political way of life. Voters approved Mississippi's 1868 constitution that formally ended slavery in the state and confirmed black voting rights, allowing Mississippi to rejoin the Union in 1870. By 1890, white Democrats had regained political control and passed a new state constitution that disfranchised black Mississippians.

Plantations, once worked by thousands of enslaved African Americans, now employed white, black, and immigrant sharecroppers and tenants. This system put small farmers in debt to landowners, exhausted Mississippi's soil, and flooded the market with cotton. Educational and professional opportunities expanded for women and African Americans, but poverty and repression persisted. New immigrant groups arrived, but they faced ongoing discrimination.

REBUILDING MISSISSIPPI

Mississippians turned to natural resources to rebuild the state's economy. After the Civil War, timber companies heavily logged in the Piney Woods region and cleared more than a million acres of Delta land, transporting lumber along new railroad lines. The Board of Mississippi Levee Commissioners created dams to control the area's frequent flooding. By the end of the nineteenth century, vast acres of rich soil were available in the Delta for farming.

Black and white farmers increasingly looked to cotton to boost their fortunes, but as many as 90 percent participated in a sharecropping system that

1868	Delegates write a state constitution, giving black men the right to vote and creating Mississippi's public school system.
1870	Mississippi rejoins the Union, and Hiram R. Revels becomes the first African American US senator.
1875	Democrats sweep state elections, and federal troops withdraw two years later, effectively ending Reconstruction in Mississippi.
1884	Nation's first public college for women founded in Columbus, known today as Mississippi University for Women.
1890	Legislators pass a new state constitution that disfranchises black voters.

51

Accordion, metal, wood, leather, and fabric, late nineteenth to early twentieth century. Dominic Biagioli brought this accordion with him when he immigrated to America in 1913 from Serra San Quirico, Italy. After arriving in the United States, Biagioli worked at Heathman Plantation, where he met his wife, Anetta. The couple later moved to Shaw, where they owned a farm and raised seven children.

left them in debt due to exorbitant rent and inflated prices at their employers' company stores. Making matters worse, cotton prices fell from around 15 cents per pound in the 1870s to 6 to 8 cents per pound in the late 1880s.

Railroad Rejuvenation

Union troops had crippled Mississippi's railroads, and in the first decade after the war, the state only added 120 miles of track. Former Confederate general P. G. T. Beauregard, as president of the New Orleans, Jackson, and Great Northern Railway, restored service to Jackson. Delaware native Henry S. McComb acquired Beauregard's railway and formed the Southern Railroad Association. In 1872 he founded McComb, Mississippi, when he moved the railroad's maintenance facilities there. The Illinois Central Railroad entered into an agreement with McComb, bringing Mississippi into one of the nation's largest rail systems. Between 1880 and 1890, state rails increased by 119 percent. In 1883 workers laid more track in Mississippi than any other state.

Commissary token, aluminum, late nineteenth to early twentieth century. Some sharecroppers were paid with tokens that could only be used at the plantation's commissary. Each token expressed its value on one side and the name of the issuing plantation on the other. This token reads "Good for 50 cents in Trade," and "M.B. Collins / Jonestown / Miss."

Patent model for screw press, wood and iron, invented by Peter Campbell, 1879. Peter Campbell was born into slavery at Joseph Davis's Hurricane Plantation in 1841. After the Civil War, he lived in a community of former slaves known as Davis Bend, in Warren County. Campbell created this model of an improved screw press, receiving a US patent for the design on April 1, 1879.

SEIZING NEW OPPORTUNITIES

Mississippi rejoined the Union in 1870 amid a whirlwind of social changes. After the Civil War, more than 430,000 formerly enslaved Mississippians made the transition to freedom, but legal freedom did not guarantee equality—economic repression, social customs, and discriminatory laws prolonged racial inequality.

Many African Americans drew on agricultural skills to become sharecroppers or tenant farmers. Others found work as domestics, railroad laborers, dockworkers, and blacksmiths. Entrepreneurs, black and white, adopted technological advancements in news media. After the Civil War, only fourteen newspapers remained active in Mississippi, but by 1900 more than sixty daily and weekly papers were available across the state. Printed in 1867, the *Vicksburg Colored Citizen* was the first periodical in Mississippi published by African Americans. Hiram Revels's paper, the *Southwestern Christian Advocate*, ran a

column called "Lost Friends" that featured messages from people searching for loved ones separated by slavery.

Mississippi established a public school framework with the passage of the 1868 Constitution. African Americans and women attended new public and private schools that educated students from elementary to college level. However, the majority of the state's population lived in rural areas where schools did not yet exist. An 1878 law mandated segregation, saying, "White and colored children shall not be taught in the same schoolhouse." The 1890 Constitution codified segregated public education. At the time of its passage, 55 percent of Mississippi's public school pupils were African American.

RETURN TO THE UNION

Masonic apron, leather with silk embroidery threads, cotton cords, cotton lining, and metallic trim, late nineteenth century. Thomas W. Stringer formed the state's first African American Masonic lodge in 1867. Men wore the chapter's symbols on ceremonial aprons that marked their membership in this fraternal society.

Congress oversaw nearly three years of US military occupation after the Civil War and required a new state constitution before allowing Mississippi to rejoin the United States in 1870. This 1868 document outlawed slavery and affirmed that African American men could vote. A Republican coalition of African Americans, white Mississippians, and northerners swept the 1869 and 1873

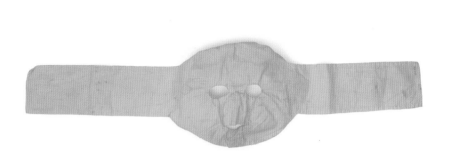

contests. Many black officials were elected, including John R. Lynch. Lynch became a state legislator in 1869, was chosen as the first African American Speaker of the Mississippi House of Representatives in 1872, and, that same year, successfully campaigned for a seat in the US Congress.

During the statewide elections of 1875, Democrats implemented the "Mississippi Plan," which appealed to white voters along racial lines and used violence to keep black voters from the polls. Anti-black violence broke out at rallies in Macon, Columbus, Vicksburg, Clinton, and other towns. Violence, stuffed ballot boxes, and intimidation tactics led to Democratic legislative victories in sixty-two of the state's seventy-four counties. Democrats impeached the black Republican lieutenant governor, and Governor Adelbert Ames resigned before being impeached. President Ulysses S. Grant's refusal to send troops and the subsequent withdrawal of remaining soldiers ensured the Mississippi Plan's success.

In 1890 Mississippi passed a new constitution that required voters to pay mandatory poll taxes and be able to read or interpret any section of the constitution. Local registrars used these restrictions to keep most African Americans and some poor white men from voting. The number of black voters dropped dramatically. When voters registered under the new constitution in 1892, only 8,615 of 150,409 eligible black men successfully registered.

KKK mask, muslin, ca. 1870–1890. Founded in Pulaski, Tennessee, in 1865, the Ku Klux Klan soon began to commit violent acts, including lynching, against African Americans and white supporters of civil rights in Mississippi. They wore masks and robes to hide their identities and heighten the drama of their activities.

Six oz. Hutchinson-stoppered bottle, glass, 1894. In the 1890s Coca-Cola could only be purchased at a limited number of stores that produced the drink by running syrup through a fountain that added carbonated soda. In 1894 Joseph A. Biedenharn (proprietor of Biedenharn and Brother candy store, founded in Vicksburg by his father and uncle) became the first bottler of Coca-Cola, using bottles like this one to distribute the beverage.

Oil lamp, brass, mid-nineteenth century. Babette and David Moses, who emigrated from Europe to Natchez in 1849, used this lamp to observe the Jewish tradition of *Shabbat* (Sabbath). Moses ran a store with his family in Natchez that sold buggies and accessories.

NEW FACES

With slavery outlawed, planters worried about retaining laborers to work the land. In 1878 Mississippi created the Board of Immigration and Agriculture to attract immigrant workers. Immigrants from Europe, Asia, and the Middle East came to Mississippi in the postwar period. Many, like Italian laborers in the Delta, took low-paying jobs on farms across the state. Others became peddlers or worked in shops, eventually purchasing their own stores. Some, like the Biedenharn and Moses families, became wealthy merchants. German, Russian, Polish, Slavonian, Italian, Lebanese, and Chinese families all journeyed to the state seeking new opportunities. The new arrivals had great impact on Mississippi's culture.

Abacus, wood and copper, before 1939. Some Chinese merchants used calculating tools like this abacus in their Mississippi shops.

Vase, porcelain with transfer print, 1903. After two years of construction, workers completed a new, 180-foot-tall Mississippi State Capitol in 1903. Legislators funded its construction with $1,093,641 in back taxes the Illinois Central Railroad owed the state. An attendee purchased this commemorative vase at the official dedication ceremony on June 3, 1903.

Promise and Peril

MISSISSIPPI WELCOMED the twentieth century as an opportunity for change. The state created new laws, including legislation in 1908 prohibiting children under twelve years old from working in factories, and supported emergent industries, including Biloxi's seafood canneries. Soaring timber production created boomtowns like Hattiesburg and Laurel. Spurred by industrial development, Jackson's population tripled from 1900 to 1918. The state government enacted reforms to improve public health care and transportation networks.

However, these changes did not help all Mississippians, and the continuation of white authority through racial and economic domination prevented further progress. Women struggled to gain the right to vote. Few African Americans benefited from social and economic legislation. The Great Mississippi Flood of 1927 decimated crops and forced black refugees to camp on narrow dirt levees for days. By the end of the 1920s, Mississippi remained mired in economic crises and racial inequality. But cars, trains, and airplanes had begun crisscrossing the state, and the first women had taken seats in the Mississippi Legislature.

1904	Timber boom ignites construction of railroads, sawmills, and new towns.
1908	Statewide prohibition of alcohol adopted prior to a federal constitutional amendment.
1916	Mississippi State Sanatorium for Tuberculosis established in Simpson County.
1917	The United States enters World War I and helps achieve Allied victory in November 1918.
1920	Nineteenth Amendment gives women the right to vote, but Mississippi's women are barred from participating in November presidential election.
1927	Massive flood along the Mississippi River displaces 185,495 state residents.

RESPONDING TO A COTTON CRISIS

Demand for raw materials during World War I spiked cotton prices to nearly one dollar per pound in 1919, but by 1921, prices plummeted to 9.8 cents per pound. At the same time, the boll weevil, which had migrated from Mexico into Mississippi in 1907, was causing more economic damage than any agricultural pest in American history. The Mississippi cotton harvest dropped

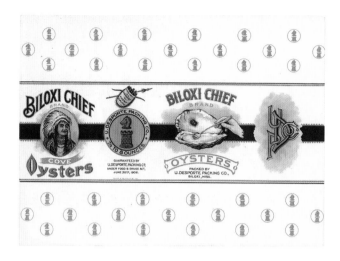

Boll weevil trap, wood and metal, manufactured by Bell Brothers, patented 1916. This trap was placed at the Dubard plantation in Grenada County. Wire brushes swept through the plants, knocking punctured bolls and insects into the trough filled with kerosene.

Label, printed by Walle & Co., 1906. This label, from the U. Desporte Packing Company in Biloxi, was made for their Biloxi Chief brand cove oysters.

from 895,000 bales in 1920 to just 604,000 in 1923. Due to the downturn, some Mississippians shifted to jobs in the seafood industry, took up truck farming, or worked in the lumber industry. Some African Americans from Mississippi joined the Great Migration toward industrial jobs and what they believed would be better lives in northern cities like Chicago and Detroit.

In 1902 Biloxi boasted twelve seafood canneries, earning the title of "Seafood Capital of the World." The "capital" was diverse—Slavic peoples, African Americans, and Louisianans of French descent all made a living by harvesting and canning oysters and shrimp from the Gulf of Mexico.

Dairy farms, creameries, and cheese plants popped up across the state during the 1920s, including the Borden Company's milk-canning facility in Starkville. Mississippi also developed a vegetable canning industry in the 1920s, but growth was slow, with only seven plants operating in 1930. Some Mississippians began truck farming, or growing large crops of fresh fruits and vegetables for shipment to distant locations. Truck farmers hired laborers on a temporary basis and paid them a low wage.

In 1870, 1,954 lumbermen worked across Mississippi, and by 1909, that number had grown to 37,178. From 1904 to 1915, Mississippi's timber industry produced more lumber than any state except Washington and Louisiana, but

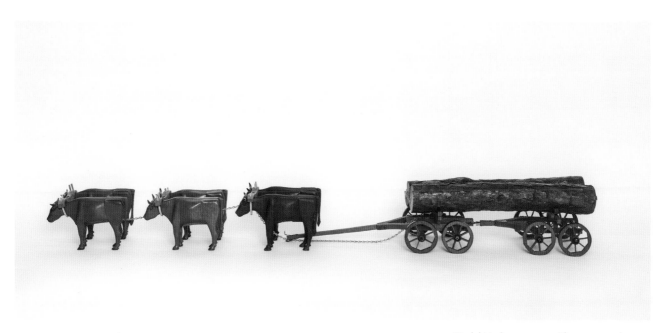

this logging boom was short-lived. By the end of the 1920s, the state's forest reserves were exhausted, and about 40,000 former lumber workers sought employment in other industries. William H. Mason explored ways to use wood from young, second-growth timber. He formed Mason Fiber Company in 1924 in Laurel and invented a durable particleboard he called "Masonite."

A MIGHTY RAMPAGE

Before 1927 levees had been constructed to prevent massive flooding of the Mississippi River. However, after months of heavy rainfall, raging floodwaters destroyed a year's worth of cotton crops, valued at $102 million. Thousands lost their homes. Many African American refugees who were told not to evacuate lived in makeshift tents on the levees. Local officials brought in the National Guard to control the refugees and force them to rebuild the levees in the flood's aftermath. The Great Mississippi River Flood of 1927 was one of the most destructive natural disasters of the twentieth century.

REFORM AND EXCLUSION

At the turn of the twentieth century, "Progressive" politicians passed laws to combat problems like poverty, alcoholism, child labor, inadequate roads, and epidemic diseases. Mississippi was the first state in the nation to implement two major Progressive reforms—primary elections (to determine each party's nominee) in 1902 and prohibition in 1908. However, Mississippi's Progressive Era leaders extended few reforms to African Americans. Lynching and other violence against black citizens surged during this period. A strong black press and new organizations such as the National Association for the Advancement of Colored People increasingly demanded equality, but gains came slowly.

A Healthier State

A number of significant advances in public health occurred at the beginning of the twentieth century. In 1903 the state's first medical school opened at the University of Mississippi. Dr. Felix Underwood, known as "the father of public health in Mississippi," spearheaded treatment initiatives for malaria, polio, and other diseases. This period saw the first vaccinations for diphtheria, whooping cough, tuberculosis, and tetanus. The first blood transfusion using modern blood-typing techniques took place in 1907. The State Hygienic Laboratory opened in 1910, and the tuberculosis sanatorium welcomed patients starting in 1916.

Founded in 1911, the Mississippi Nurses Association worked to defeat a bill "to prohibit white nurses from caring for Negro patients in Mississippi hospitals." They also lobbied for a board of nurse examiners to oversee nursing regulations. On March 14, 1914, the Nurse Practice Act became law. Bureaus of Child Hygiene and Public Health Nursing were established in 1920. In 1922 Mississippi Director of Public Health Nursing Mary Osborne developed the *Manual for Midwives*, a teaching guide and reference book that contributed to a 40 percent drop in statewide infant mortality between 1921 and 1942.

Necktie, silk crepe with cotton lining, ca. 1935. In 1911 LeRoy Percy referred to his opponent for US Senate, James K. Vardaman, and his supporters as "rednecks." A Vardaman supporter, State Senator Theodore G. Bilbo, who owned this necktie, took ownership of the term by adopting a red necktie and suspenders as his trademark look. Later, as governor, Bilbo advocated reforms such as the establishment of a tuberculosis sanatorium and the development of a state highway system. Proud of his membership in the Ku Klux Klan, Bilbo relentlessly promoted white supremacy.

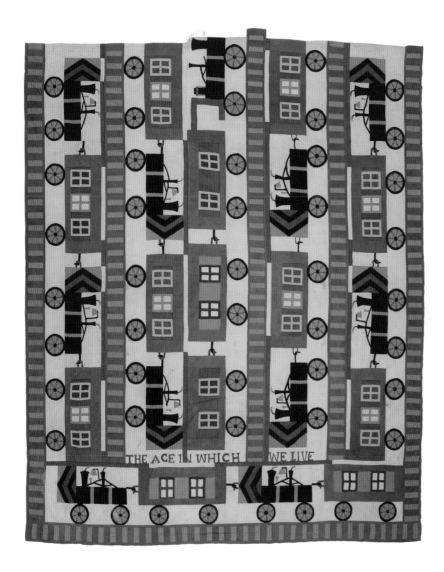

THE AGE IN WHICH WE LIVE

Mississippi license tag and holder, paper in metal and glass, issued to M. R. Martin of Franklin County for his Chevrolet, 1927.

The Age in Which We Live, cotton, quilt designed and made by Mrs. M. J. Saunders, ca. 1880s. Saunders created this quilt after her first train ride to the state's Gulf Coast. The quilt features railroad imagery, including steam engines, boxcars, and tracks.

Mississippi on the Move

The state continued to develop new and improved roads to better accommodate the latest technology in transport—the automobile. Although there were only twenty cars in Mississippi at the turn of the century, the next few decades saw widespread use of the automobile. The first state highway commission

Rebel Yell whiskey bottle, glass, ca. 1966. Alcohol still flowed in the state during Prohibition. Seeking a share of the revenue, Mississippi enacted a so-called "Black Market Tax" that enabled the state to collect sales and excise taxes on liquor brought into the state illegally. This whiskey bottle features a label that commemorates the 1966 repeal of the prohibition law in Mississippi.

formed in 1916 under Governor Theodore Bilbo. In 1930 the Mississippi River Bridge at Vicksburg opened.

Trains roared across the state, with more than forty-five railroads at the time. The logging industry funded the construction of new rail lines. From the 1880s through the early 1900s, workers cleared land and laid track for the Mobile, Jackson, and Kansas City Railroad and the Gulf and Ship Island Railroad. Towns like Hattiesburg, Laurel, Picayune, and Wiggins quickly popped up along the rails.

Payne Field, Mississippi's first airport, opened outside West Point in 1917. The US Army Air Service used it as a training facility until 1920. Mississippi aviation expanded as crop dusting became an important means of pest control during the boll weevil infestation of the 1920s. The growth of commercial aviation sparked the construction of airports across the state, including Jackson's Hawkins Field, established in 1928.

Winning the Vote

At the outset of the twentieth century, women could not vote in Mississippi or most of the United States. Organizations including the segregated Mississippi Woman Suffrage Association, organized by Nellie Nugent Somerville, and the Women's Christian Temperance Union (WCTU), led by Frances Willard, called for sweeping social and political changes. WCTU campaigned in Mississippi during the 1880s against the evils of liquor, helping to secure statewide prohibition in 1908. Suffragettes appealed to the Mississippi Legislature in 1914 and 1918 to support a federal amendment giving women the right to vote. Despite these efforts, legislators voted to reject the Nineteenth Amendment on March 29, 1920. Less than five months later, after thirty-six other states supported it, the amendment went into effect nationwide. Suffragettes Nellie Nugent Somerville and Belle Kearney became the first Mississippi women to win elections and serve in the legislature. Mississippi formally ratified the Nineteenth Amendment in 1984, nearly sixty-four years after it originally became law.

MISSISSIPPIANS AND WORLD WAR I

Some Mississippians opposed American involvement in "foreign wars," while other supported it. Senator James K. Vardaman voiced the concerns of many small farmers and poor people, who feared that the burden of fighting would fall on their shoulders. Vardaman was one of only six US senators to vote against the Declaration of War. He also opposed drafting African Americans, noting that "arrogant strutting representatives of the black soldiery" could jeopardize postwar white supremacy. The state's other senator, John Sharp Williams, advocated an inclusive draft to distribute sacrifices between both races.

After the United States entered World War I in 1917, the Hattiesburg Commerce Club approached the US Army and offered land for a proposed training camp. Military officials accepted, and Camp Shelby opened on July 18, 1917. Today, the base serves more than 100,000 military personnel annually.

Mississippians at home helped with the war effort. Some joined the Red Cross, while others purchased Liberty Bonds to help cover the costs of the war. The government urged all Americans to conserve food for soldiers abroad.

By the war's end, 32,527 white Mississippians and 25,048 black Mississippians served in segregated units. Most African American soldiers were assigned to support roles, loading and transporting supplies, clearing debris, and burying corpses.

World War I US Model 1917 helmet, steel, ca. 1917. American helmets featured a shallow steel dome with a leather chinstrap. Ben F. Kerr of Moorhead, Mississippi, trained at Camp Shelby and wore this helmet during his service in France.

Portrait of C. L. Dees, oil on canvas, by Francilla Day, 1970. In the early twentieth century, the general store was a place to purchase goods for the home, send and receive mail, and catch up with friends and family. This portrait depicts the proprietor of C. L. Dees General Merchandising Store in Vancleave, Mississippi. Dees ran the store and its mailroom from the 1920s until his death in 1963.

Bridging Hardship

GREAT DEPRESSION, NEW DEAL, AND WORLD WAR II (1928–1945)

T HE GREAT DEPRESSION compounded poverty in Mississippi, where most people still lived as tenant farmers or sharecroppers, with limited access to education, news, or health care. Federal programs paid farmers not to plant. Crop prices rose, but landowners idled plots worked by sharecroppers and then evicted them. Many displaced African Americans moved to the North, continuing the Great Migration. The 1927 flood and excessive logging left vast stretches of land barren and scarred, from the Delta to the Piney Woods. Between 1929 and 1933, industrial jobs fell from 52,000 to 28,000, half the money deposited in banks evaporated, and farm revenue collapsed.

By 1930 Mississippians earned only about one-third of the national average income. Two years later, unemployment among working-age Mississippians reached 27 percent. The federal New Deal created programs like the Works Progress Administration (WPA), Civilian Conservation Corps (CCC), and Tennessee Valley Authority (TVA) that put people—mostly whites—to work, brought electrification, nurtured the environment, and helped feed and clothe impoverished citizens.

Thousands of black and white Mississippians fought for freedom abroad during World War II (1941–1945), causing many returning service members to question racial inequality at home. Women entered the workforce as military spending remade towns like Pascagoula, Biloxi, and Moss Point.

AGRICULTURE TO INDUSTRY

Some 95 percent of Mississippi Delta farmers in 1930 did not own the land they worked. Sharecroppers—almost 30,000 between 1940 and 1945 alone— left the fields to support the war effort or for better paying jobs in emerging

1929	Cotton prices fell to six cents per pound, deepening the Great Depression in Mississippi.
1932	Some 27 percent of working-age Mississippians were jobless.
1934	Parts of northeast Mississippi became some of the first rural areas in the country to get electricity.
1936	CCC completed construction of Tishomingo State Park.
1942	Wages from new industrial plants rose to $17.9 million—fifteen times what they were in 1939.
1945	Over 200,000 Mississippians served in World War II.

Evening gown, satin, ca. 1935. In 1935 Shelby's LeFrance "Sis" Boyette became the first Miss Mississippi to compete for Miss America. Her family splurged to purchase this gown from a Greenville department store.

industries like oil drilling. By 1929 seventeen large oil firms—including Gulf and Shell—had registered to drill for oil in Mississippi. However, it was not until 1939 that a Mississippi scientist working on a New Deal project in Yazoo County discovered the Tinsley Oil Field, uncapping the first commercial petroleum well in the state.

In 1930 only 1.5 percent of Mississippi's farm homes had electricity. The federal government's rural electrification program, which began in Tupelo in 1934, led to increased mechanization, creating more non-farming industries. Tupelo became the "First TVA City," and Alcorn County formed the first electric power cooperative. By 1940 electricity lit up 27,670 farm homes in Mississippi.

FIGHTING THE TIDE

Spearheaded by President Franklin D. Roosevelt, the New Deal established federal relief programs during the Great Depression including the WPA, CCC, and TVA. As chair of the Senate Finance Committee, Mississippi senator Pat Harrison played a key role in the passage of New Deal legislation, including the Social Security Act in 1935, which required the state to establish its first professionally staffed welfare agency. Mississippi's Ellen S. Woodward served as the director of women's and professional projects, overseeing federal work relief programs for women and the arts during the New Deal before she resigned in 1938 to become a member of the Social Security Board.

Between 1935 and 1940, New Deal agencies provided work for almost 75,000 Mississippians. The WPA alone employed as many as 40,000 Mississippians between 1938 and 1940. But not everyone in Mississippi benefited from New Deal programs. State administrators relegated the relatively few African Americans they hired to low-paying, menial jobs, and segregation excluded blacks from the new CCC-built state parks. Some New Deal policies, like the Agricultural Adjustment Agency, which offered landowners money to reduce crop production, forced many families off land they had worked for generations. Later, the Farm Security Administration gave loans that helped some sharecroppers to buy their land.

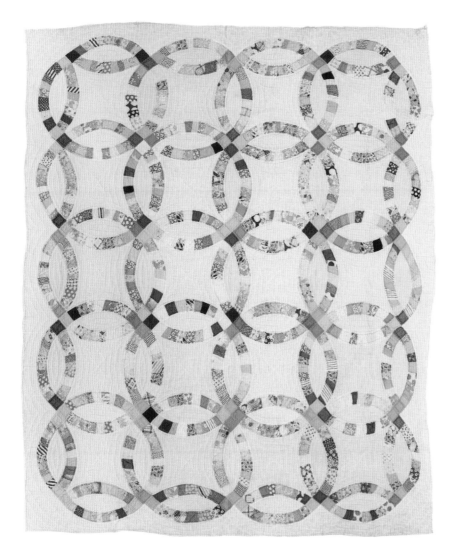

Former head of the Mississippi WPA, Governor Hugh White proposed the Balance Agriculture with Industry program, which offered incentives to industrial plants such as local financing and worker training programs. Wages from jobs at new plants, such as Ingalls Shipbuilding in Pascagoula, rose from $1.4 million in 1939 to $17.9 million in 1942.

Bed quilt, "Double Wedding Ring" pattern, cotton with cotton feed sacks, ca. 1930–1939. During a time of widespread poverty, women repurposed cotton-cloth feed and flour sacks to create quilts, clothing, and tablecloths. Grace Davis of Summit recalled, "After a year or two manufacturers began to put [feed] into printed sacks. That also meant some member[s] of the family would get a new shirt or a new dress. . . . It took [three] sacks to make a dress."

Sharecropper, oil on canvas, by Marie A. Hull, 1938. Summit native Marie Hull painted a series of Mississippi sharecroppers during the Great Depression. She stated, "I find that people who live close to the earthly, fundamental things usually have more character in their faces."

Making Mississippians Healthier

Funds from New Deal programs supported efforts to combat preventable diseases. Public health nurses brought care and instruction in sanitary practices to rural areas. In the 1930s and 1940s, diseases including pellagra, syphilis, and tuberculosis continued to plague the state. Nurses, like Sunflower County's Janie Clara Breckenridge (who worked from 1926 to 1972), conducted rural clinics at schools, churches, and country stores. In an era when most mothers gave birth at home, Breckenridge delivered some 1,500 babies.

THE FIGHT FOR FREEDOM

World War II transformed Mississippi's physical and social landscape. The army built thirty-six new bases and airfields. An influx of trainees from across the United States, including segregated units of black and white troops, quickly filled these facilities. By war's end, more than 10 percent of Mississippi's total population had served in the military. Over 4,000 died. Men and women filled new jobs at bases and military factories. Mississippians doubled their incomes—which remained half of the national average—and urban populations exploded in towns like Pascagoula and Meridian.

Serving Segregated America

Thousands of black Mississippians enlisted in the armed forces. James Rundles, a Jackson native, became the first African American to enlist in the US Marine Corps. Returning black soldiers questioned whether the United States really embodied the ideals of freedom and justice they had defended abroad. Their "Double V" campaign called for victory against tyranny abroad and racism at home. Japanese American soldiers arrived at Camp Shelby to find they were excluded from both the white and black USO clubs. One Hattiesburg man, Earl Finch, created a USO for these soldiers, and the community gradually came to accept them.

Model crib, wood with wire, designed by nurse Caroline Benoist, ca. 1936. This crib protected babies from flies and mosquitoes, which carried disease.

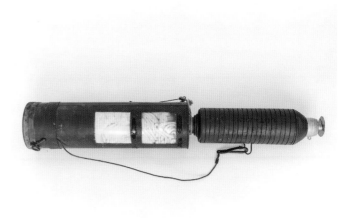

Prisoners of War

The military shipped 20,000 prisoners of war (POWs), mostly captured Germans or Italians, to four major prison camps in Mississippi. The camps offered medical care, movies, and other services. In 1944 POWs were put to work picking cotton in the Delta and timbering in the Piney Woods. At Camp Clinton, they constructed a one-square-mile model of the Mississippi River basin to study flood patterns. Most POWs remained for almost a year after the fighting ended to supply workers for the labor-starved state.

Sacrifice, Support, and Transitions at Home

Mississippians at home sacrificed to support the war effort. Food rationing included "Meatless Mondays" and "Wheatless Wednesdays." With rubber diverted to the war front, car tires became scarce, and the state made stealing tires a felony. Women cut patterns and sewed uniforms, raised funds for the Red Cross, and went to work at military factories and bases. Women filled jobs traditionally held by men, challenging long-standing gender roles in the workplace. For many, it was their first experience working outside the home.

Dinner plate, "Patio" design, ceramic, manufactured by Mikado China, ca. 1940. This plate was once owned by A. M. E. Logan, who was known as the "Mother of the Jackson Civil Rights Movement." She housed and fed many civil rights workers, including Freedom Riders. Logan moved to Jackson in the 1940s and held a number of positions within the state and local NAACP organizations.

Forging Ahead

CIVIL RIGHTS, DIVERSIFICATION, AND INNOVATION
(1946–PRESENT)

AFRICAN AMERICANS' STRUGGLE for civil rights dominated the 1950s and 1960s. The world watched Mississippi as the Civil Rights Movement brought racial segregation, voting rights, and economic inequality into public discussion. Activists pushed the federal government to begin dismantling some of the barriers facing black citizens. With Jim Crow segregation and disfranchisement challenged, protesters turned to economic injustice. A major shift in party politics also characterized this period, as white Mississippians began moving from the Democratic to the Republican Party.

Mississippi's economy and population changed significantly. The state's manufacturing, service, and high-tech industries grew and shrank over time. As the number of agricultural jobs decreased, many people moved from rural areas to cities. The century-long Great Migration continued, leading to a decline in the state's black population, while the number of immigrants increased.

STRUGGLE FOR EQUALITY

African Americans refused to accept continued inequality and injustice, sparking the modern Civil Rights Movement. Throughout the twentieth century, thousands of activists worked to secure equal rights through petitions and protests. The fight demanded sacrifices and risks.

The National Association for the Advancement of Colored People (NAACP) had been working in Mississippi for years. In 1954 Medgar Evers became the first fulltime Mississippi field secretary for the NAACP. He investigated cases of racial violence and intimidation, worked with the media, and

1948   Mississippi delegates walk out of Democratic National Convention, in protest of the party's civil rights platform.

1954   Medgar Evers becomes first fulltime Mississippi field secretary for the NAACP.

1965   Congress passes Voting Rights Act, outlawing literacy tests and providing federal registrars and observers.

1970   All state school districts desegregate.

1986   Mike Espy elected to US Congress, becoming the first African American to represent Mississippi at the federal level since the 1880s.

2005   Hurricane Katrina causes $75 billion in damage along the Mississippi Gulf Coast.

Membership badge, bronze and ribbon, manufactured by Crafters Inc., 1956. Wirt Yerger Jr. wore this badge at the 1956 Republican National Convention, where he was chair of the Mississippi delegation.

organized protests and local NAACP branches. Facing entrenched opposition and grave danger, Evers never relented in his fight for justice. He was assassinated at his home in Jackson in 1963.

A number of grass roots organizations emerged during the Civil Rights Movement to initiate programs and organize volunteers. One of those was the Student Nonviolent Coordinating Committee (SNCC), which formed in 1960. In 1961 SNCC staffer Bob Moses started a voter registration project in McComb, where he recruited Hollis Watkins, the first black Mississippian to join the civil rights group. In 1962 Fannie Lou Hamer joined SNCC, working with fellow Mississippi native Charles McLaurin in the Delta. Several civil rights groups joined together to form the Council of Federated Organizations (COFO) in Mississippi. In 1964 COFO spearheaded an education, healthcare, and voting rights program in Mississippi called Freedom Summer. Hamer helped organize voter registration initiatives during Freedom Summer and joined the Mississippi Freedom Democratic Party, working for equality until her death in 1977.

Years of demonstrations and televised violence against civil rights protesters sparked federal action. In 1964 and 1965, Congress passed landmark civil rights legislation to prohibit discrimination in housing and public facilities and to secure voting rights. The number of African American registered voters swelled from just under 7 percent of eligible residents in 1964 to nearly 60 percent in 1968. The determination of ordinary people, forcing the federal government to uphold the rights of all Americans as promised in the US Constitution, illuminated a path toward greater racial equality in Mississippi.

THE MODERN POLITICAL PARTIES EMERGE

The shift of southern Democratic politicians and voters to the Republican Party took place over several decades. In the 1870s the Republican Party advanced equal rights for African Americans as part of Reconstruction. White factions in Mississippi united under the Democratic Party to overthrow Republican rule and end black voting rights, creating a one-party system.

The New Deal brought African Americans into the Democratic Party after 1932. In 1948 party leaders at the Democratic National Convention expressed support for civil rights, and Mississippi's delegates walked out in protest. Passage of the 1964 Civil Rights Act caused many white Mississippians to reconsider their support of the national Democratic Party. Over time, the more conservative Republican position appealed to many white Mississippians, and the Republican Party became dominant in state politics.

Mississippi Republicans

In 1955 Wirt Yerger Jr. started a Young Republicans chapter in Mississippi, joining several existing party factions. By 1960 his coalition was recognized as the official Mississippi Republican Party. Yerger joined with supporters of Republican presidential candidate Dwight D. Eisenhower and began fielding candidates in state and local elections in the 1960s. As longtime Democratic incumbents retired, a new generation of Republicans won their seats. In 1991 voters elected Kirk Fordice, the first Republican governor since 1873. In 2011 Republicans gained control of both houses of the state legislature for the first time since 1875.

Mississippi Democrats

After signing the Civil Rights Act of 1964, President Lyndon B. Johnson said, "I think we just delivered the South to the Republican Party for a long time to come." Democratic support of civil rights hurt the party's future in Mississippi. However, the Democratic platform appealed to newly enfranchised black voters. In 1968 Robert Clark Jr. became the first African American elected to the Mississippi House of Representatives in the twentieth century. In 1987 Democrat Mike Espy became the first black member of the US Congress from Mississippi since the 1880s.

Evening gown, silk/taffeta with chiffon overlay, ca. 1976. Democrat Evelyn Gandy became Mississippi's first woman lieutenant governor. She wore this dress during her inaugural reception in 1976.

RISING FROM THE RUINS

Natural disasters have inflicted widespread devastation to people, property, and land in Mississippi. Manmade disasters have also affected the state in adverse ways. In the aftermath of catastrophe, Mississippians unite to recover and rebuild.

In 1969 Hurricane Camille caused approximately 150 deaths and the equivalent of over $6 billion in damage. In 2005 Hurricane Katrina claimed more than 238 lives and severely damaged 160,000 Mississippi homes with winds reaching 175 miles per hour and a storm surge of thirty feet. Tornadoes frequently batter communities throughout the state—forty storms occurred in

Clock, brass, manufactured by Quartz, ca. 2000. This clock stopped when twelve feet of water flooded Edmond Boudreaux's Biloxi home during Hurricane Katrina.

2014 alone. In 1966 a violent tornado struck central Mississippi, including Hinds, Rankin, Scott, and Leake Counties, its winds exceeding 260 miles per hour, killing fifty-seven people. A similar twister, with winds topping 205 miles per hour, devastated Smithville on April 27, 2011, destroying more than 200 homes and killing fifteen.

Manmade disasters pose new challenges. In 2010 the *Deepwater Horizon* offshore oil rig exploded, killing eleven workers and eventually spewing 4.9 million barrels of oil into waters along the Gulf Coast. The spill, which took months to stop, threatened Mississippi's commercial fishing and tourism industries. A large-scale cleanup effort removed oil from the state's forty-four-mile coastline.

Slot machine, manufactured by International Game Technology, 2005.

BUILDING A NEW MISSISSIPPI

As the state advanced through the 2000s, leaders focused on economic growth and employment, which remain among the state's greatest challenges. The percentage of Mississippi residents living in poverty has dropped dramatically, from 55 percent in the 1950s to 24 percent by 2013. However, 37.7 percent of African American families lived in poverty that year, and Mississippians' personal incomes in the early twenty-first century still ranked among the lowest in the nation.

Mississippi also lagged behind other states in public health issues, though in 2011 the state led the nation in childhood immunization rates. The 2012 Mississippi Health Care Industry Zone Act sought to expand access to health care and the number of related jobs. Health care employment rose from nearly 87,000 jobs in 2003 to more than 108,000 by 2013.

Unique cultural, historic, and recreational attractions continue to draw hundreds of thousands of tourists each year. In the late twentieth century, Mississippi's tourism and gaming industries grew, contributing millions of dollars in tax revenue to the state. The passage of the Mississippi Gaming Control Act of 1990 paved the way for legal gambling, with the first casinos opening in 1992. Tax revenue from gaming increased from $44.4 million in 1993 to more than $250 million in 2015.

Mississippi workers make products as varied as food, textiles, automobiles, and electrical equipment. In 2015 the food and beverage industry employed more than 30,000 people in 250 manufacturing plants for companies like Borden, Sanderson Farms, and Uncle Ben's Rice. High-tech production facilities, like Peavey Electronics in Meridian and Hancock County's Stennis Space Center, contributed to the state's 240,000 manufacturing jobs in 2000,

matching an industrial employment high set in 1978. Because of the loss of jobs overseas, however, this figure fell to just over 140,000 in 2014. Completed in 2003, the Nissan Motor Company plant in Canton employed 6,000 people a decade later. In 2014 the Toyota Motor Corporation's Blue Springs plant manufactured more than 7,500 Corollas that shipped to eighteen countries around the world, supporting over 2,000 jobs in the state. Ingalls Shipbuilding in Pascagoula employed over 11,000 people in 2014, making it the state's largest manufacturing employer. As of 2015, more than 70 percent of all ships in the US Navy had been built at the 800-acre facility.

Miss America crown, metal with rhinestones, manufactured by Marcel Boucher & Cie., 1958. In 1958 Biloxi native Mary Ann Mobley became the first Miss Mississippi to win the Miss America pageant. Mobley went on to act in film, television, and Broadway productions before her death in 2014.

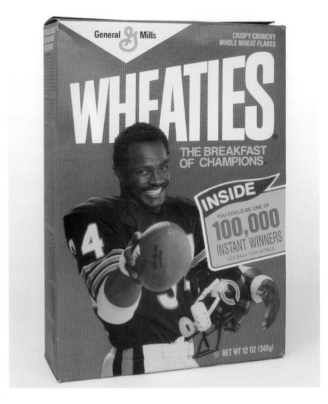

Spice box, stainless steel, ca. 1971. Spice boxes hold six or seven frequently used spices and are kept near stoves in Indian kitchens for easy access. This spice box was given to Seetha Srinivasan by her grandmother, who used it in her home in India.

Wheaties cereal box, cardboard, 1987. Nicknamed "Sweetness," Walter Payton grew up in Columbia, Mississippi. He was a two-time All-American football player at Jackson State University. Following college, he played for the Chicago Bears and was one of the greatest running backs of all time. In 1987 he became the first NFL player to appear on a Wheaties cereal box. The Pro Football Hall of Fame inducted Payton in 1996 shortly before his death from cancer at the age of forty-six.

THE PEOPLE OF MISSISSIPPI

Throughout the state's history, people from all walks of life have shaped today's Mississippi. Community activists, artisans, entrepreneurs, political figures, entertainers, athletes, and everyday citizens all contribute to Mississippi's story. Immigrant groups remain a vital part of the state's cultural and economic fabric—as of 2013, one out of every fifty Mississippians was foreign-born. Chinese, Italian, German, Lebanese, and Greek settlers, as well as Jewish people from other countries, migrated to the state throughout the nineteenth and early twentieth centuries. In more recent years, settlers from Asia and Latin America immigrated to Mississippi in increasing numbers. The heartbeat of the state, people from diverse backgrounds draw upon important cultural traditions, while utilizing talent and ingenuity to benefit the broader community.

Landscape, embroidery in lid of wooden box, by Wilda Cabrera Cartagena, 1980. Cartagena and her husband, Juan, immigrated to Morton, Mississippi, from Chile in 1979. Wilda wove intricate tapestries that interpreted Chile, while furniture maker Juan Cartagena practiced woodworking.

THE SOUL OF OUR STATE

The art that speaks most clearly, explicitly, directly and passionately from its own place of origin will remain the longest understood.
—EUDORA WELTY, 1954

Untitled, painted clay with corn kernels and cotton, by James "Son Ford" Thomas, mid-twentieth century. Leland artist and musician Son Thomas excelled as a sculptor and guitarist. Thomas used native clay and found objects to create artwork, at times incorporating actual human teeth into his popular clay skulls. He is known worldwide as a bluesman.

The roots of creativity run deep in Mississippi, flowering from the heart of family, a stimulating physical environment, and a history of struggle. Creativity was always here, even through slavery, wars, economic setbacks, and racial inequality. A sense of place connects artists to our shared history. The expressions of the earliest musicians, artists, and writers came from the soul—because there were songs and images and stories to be shared.

Today's artists come from a long line of gifted forebears. Musicians, artists, and writers from Mississippi are celebrated worldwide. Their award-winning work tackles complex issues and pioneers new styles and forms. These talented people have enriched Mississippi, crafting a unique tradition of creativity and a rich cultural legacy.

MUSIC: ROOTED IN MISSISSIPPI

Mississippi is widely acknowledged as the birthplace of America's music. Local musicians grew up surrounded by music—at church and at home. In the early 1800s, black and white Mississippians worshiped and sang together, combining African and European musical traditions. With this foundation in place, Mississippi musicians created the genres of blues, country, and rock and roll. The original sound and songwriting talent emerging from Mississippi met both critical and popular success.

Gospel quartets and choirs built upon nineteenth-century spirituals and hymns. Record companies began to release albums by African American preachers and gospel artists in the 1920s. Gospel developed further as ministers combined preaching and singing. In the late 1940s, groups like the Five Blind Boys of Mississippi and the Staple Singers (whose patriarch is from Drew) added four-part harmonies, instrumentation, African rhythms, and movement. The

Dobro guitar, wood, mother of pearl, and metal, manufactured ca. 1932. Dobro, now owned by Gibson, began producing guitars in 1928, though the word *Dobro* has commonly been used to describe a wood-bodied, single-cone resonator guitar, regardless of maker. Bluesman Tobe Hudson of Gholson ordered this guitar from Sears, Roebuck, and Co. in 1932.

Metropolitan Opera ticket for *Aida*, paper, 1985. Known for roles in *Il Trovatore*, *Antony and Cleopatra*, and *Aida*, Leontyne Price won more than a dozen Grammy Awards and received the Presidential Medal of Freedom in 1964.

Canton Spirituals and the Mississippi Mass Choir are long-standing, internationally acclaimed groups that continue to perform.

The blues began as the state's enslaved people labored in the cottonfields, passing time by clapping and chanting. By the 1890s these "field hollers" were combined with European traditional music, improvisation, and other elements to create the blues. Blues instruments are diverse but often include the harmonica, guitar, keyboards, and drums, along with vocals that cover a multitude of themes like love, hardships, money, and religion. Early blues musicians including Charley Patton, Eddie "Son" House, and Robert Johnson played juke joints in the Mississippi Delta, swapping songs and meeting mentors. In the 1920s Big Bill Broonzy of Scott, Willie Dixon of Vicksburg, and other musicians migrated north. Sonny Boy Williamson and Big Walter Horton formed blues bands in the Delta. Muddy Waters of Rolling Fork and B.B. King of Berclair refined electric blues in Chicago and Memphis. Beginning in the 1940s, musicians like "Big Boy" Crudup of Forest and Guitar Slim of Greenwood developed rhythm and blues. Bobby Rush and Dorothy Moore, both of Jackson, are living legends of R&B.

In the late 1920s, Meridian native Jimmie Rodgers pioneered the country music style, fusing blues, gospel, jazz, and folk music into his distinctive songs. Many highly acclaimed country stars and songwriters hail from Mississippi. Conway Twitty of Friars Point produced more than fifty number one hits during his long career. Tammy Wynette, a native of Itawamba County, sold in excess of thirty million records after moving to Nashville in 1966. Topping the charts for more than twenty years, Charley Pride of Sledge stands out as a successful African American country artist. Other Mississippi country stars include Marty Stuart of Philadelphia, Bobbie Gentry of Greenwood, O. B. McClinton of Senatobia, Mickey Gilley of Natchez, Faith Hill of Star, and LeAnn Rimes of Pearl.

Clarksdale native Ike Turner wrote "Rocket '88," often considered the first rock and roll record. Bo Diddley of Magnolia also helped found rock and roll. Beginning in the 1950s, he crafted a unique sound, built on a distinctive, Caribbean-influenced rhythm that became known as the "Bo Diddley beat." Elvis Presley of Tupelo combined blues, gospel, pop, and country styles into his music. In 1956 his record "Heartbreak Hotel" reached number one, and Elvis became known internationally as the "King of Rock and Roll." In 1986 Jerry Lee

Lewis of Nesbit was the first person inducted into the Rock and Roll Hall of Fame. Pascagoula native Jimmy Buffett takes a more laid-back approach through his island-inspired songs.

Contributions to Jazz and Classical Music

New Orleans nurtured jazz, which developed from a mixture of African, European, ragtime, and other kinds of music. Mississippians Milt Hinton, Lester Young, and others were pioneers of this improvisational style. Mose Allison of Tippo became an important twentieth-century jazz pianist, singer, and songwriter, while Cassandra Wilson of Jackson continues to compose and dazzle audiences with her vocals.

Mississippians have also contributed to classical music, including notable composers William Grant Still of Woodville and Milton Babbitt of Jackson. Soprano Leontyne Price of Laurel became one of the most recognized stars in the world of opera.

TRADITIONAL CRAFTS

Visual art in Mississippi began in prehistoric times when Native Americans crafted utilitarian and trade objects with great skill and beauty, a tradition that continues today. Throughout history, Mississippians have created items for use in everyday life from readily available materials, many of which come straight from nature, like local wood, river cane, or clay. Craftspeople have honed their skills in quilting, sewing, basketmaking, woodworking, pottery, glassworking, blacksmithing, metalworking, and other art forms. Traditional crafts have evolved over the years, with artisans now creating fine crafts that are highly collectible and valued as artwork. In many cases, the line between "fine craft" and "fine art" is blurred, as artists have adopted traditional techniques to realize their visions.

Basket, dyed and woven swamp cane, by L. Wallace, ca. 1975–1984. The maker of this colorful basket used commercial dyes in orange, red, black, and green, as well as natural swamp cane. This design is sometimes called a snake basket because the diamonds represent the eastern diamondback rattlesnake.

Quilt, "Octagonal Star" pattern, cotton, ca. 1880–1890. This quilt was handmade by Sallie Bailey Bryant, her sister Ellen Bailey, or the aunt who reared them, Ellen Lea Bailey, of Oxford. Pieced and quilted by hand, the quilt was passed down through the Bailey family.

Quilting was one way Mississippians, free and enslaved, expressed their creativity while creating treasured family heirlooms. Early quilts featured an array of patterns and were made from a variety of materials, including imported cloth, fabric scraps, and feed sacks. Port Gibson's Hystercine Rankin and Yazoo City's Sarah Mary Taylor were standout quilters in the late twentieth century. Gwendolyn A. Magee of Jackson created quilts with original imagery and intricate stitching that conveyed narratives related to African American history and civil rights.

MISSISSIPPI'S VISUAL ARTS

Explorers and colonists arrived in the seventeenth and eighteenth centuries, bringing their artistic traditions with them. Alexander Wilson, a Scottish immigrant and ornithologist, was among the first European artists to visit Natchez, arriving in 1810. Wealthy settlers built elegant homes, which they furnished with decorative objects and paintings by the nation's finest artists, but Mississippi artists were rare until the 1840s. James Tooley Jr., who was born in Mississippi in 1816, achieved national recognition as a miniaturist, and Edwin Lyon began sculpting marble busts and gravestones in Natchez. Henry Norman, prominent nineteenth-century photographer, recorded the people and places of Natchez for more than forty years. Portrait painter Thomas Healy moved to Port Gibson in the 1840s, following his studies in Boston and Paris.

Vessel, glazed clay, by George E. Ohr, ca. 1900–1906. George Ohr, known as the "mad potter of Biloxi," was an innovative artist who worked in the late nineteenth and early twentieth centuries. He created thin-walled, whimsically shaped, glazed vessels that were unappreciated at the time, but were later praised by art critics from around the country.

Untitled, ceramic with glaze on stick, by Mildred Nungester Wolfe, mid-twentieth century. Wolfe Studio, founded in 1946 by Mildred and her husband, Karl Wolfe, still produces ceramic work today.

After the Civil War, artist traveler William Aiken Walker of Charleston, South Carolina, recorded people and places of the Delta and Gulf Coast. Impressionist Kate Freeman Clark of Holly Springs studied with William Merritt Chase between 1896 and 1902 and became highly successful in the art world of New York before returning to Mississippi. Arthur Putnam of Waveland created dynamic animal figures that garnered attention and praise in Paris, where he moved in the early 1920s. Raised in Bay St. Louis, African American sculptor Richmond Barthé depicted the human figure in bronzes that can be found in major collections across the country.

A Community for Artists

Twentieth-century artists laid the groundwork for artists currently working in the state by forming long-lasting artist groups, teaching, and experimenting with style and materials. In 1911 Jackson artist Bessie Cary Lemly organized the Mississippi Art Association (later the Mississippi Museum of Art). Karl Wolfe served as director of nearby Allison's Art Colony. Marie Hull painted in Jackson for more than sixty years, teaching generations of students in her home. Richard Beadle photographed twentieth-century black life in Jackson for more than fifty years. Ellsworth Woodward founded the Gulf Coast Art Association in 1926, and Peter Anderson formed Shearwater Pottery at Ocean Springs in 1928. Lee and Pup McCarty founded an art pottery business in Merigold in 1954. Greenville sculptor Leon Koury was director of the WPA Mississippi Art Project, and he taught and worked in the Delta for more than thirty years. Artist Caroline Compton founded the Vicksburg Art Association in 1961.

Art in Modern Times

Dusti Bongé of Biloxi was Mississippi's first true modern artist, and her work was shown at Betty Parsons Gallery in New York from 1954 until 1974. Oxford artist Theora Hamblett's visionary paintings also caught the attention of Parsons, who helped promote the artist and her work. Late twentieth-century artists from Mississippi went on to successful careers in the arts outside the state: Bill

Monarch Butterflies on Horn Island, watercolor on paper, by Walter Inglis Anderson, mid-twentieth century. Renowned Ocean Springs artist Walter Anderson began camping alone on Horn Island in 1947, producing hundreds of watercolors there.

Untitled, cotton and metallic thread on linen, by Ethel Wright Mohamed, ca. 1980. Mohamed created more than 125 memory pictures with narrative scenes from her life, each one embroidered by hand. "Listen, as I pull the needle through the material, it makes music. I think that's the reason I'm so enchanted with it."—Ethel Wright Mohamed

Dunlap, Sam Gilliam, Valerie Jaudon, Ed McGowin, James Seawright, and many others. Contemporary photographer William Eggleston achieved worldwide acclaim when his work became the first color photography acquired by the Museum of Modern Art in New York City. Marshall Bouldin III of Clarksdale received international recognition as a portrait painter, and his son Jason Bouldin, of Oxford, carries on the tradition. The visual art scene of Mississippi remains vibrant in the twenty-first century, with hundreds of professional artists and teachers working and exhibiting across the state and country.

STORYTELLING: A WAY OF LIFE

A robust oral tradition matured in Mississippi. Native Americans passed down their history and religious practices. Generations of settlers shared memories and told tales, as future writers sat at their feet. People told stories wherever they gathered—front porches, church pews, or town squares. Religious practice provided material, and many writers used biblical themes and characters. Whether fact or fiction, stories injected excitement into small-town life.

Early Literature

In the eighteenth century, settlers began publishing their writings. Augustus Baldwin Longstreet, Joseph Beckham Cobb, and others printed "southwestern humor," colorful tales of frontier life in the decades before the Civil War. Men and women wrote poetry, Gothic novels, historical and romantic fiction, histories, and travel volumes. Sarah Dorsey, Eliza Dupuy, and Catherine Ware Warfield published novels in the 1860s.

Emerging in the 1870s, "local color" writers like Irwin Russell used regional characteristics and dialects. Activist authors penned essays on slavery, civil rights, and other issues. Newspapers published many stories, often serializing the popular ones.

Flowering of Southern Letters

In the 1920s Mississippi fiction writers began achieving worldwide acclaim. Their distinctly southern experiences resonated with universal human themes. William Faulkner and Stark Young led with *The Sound and the Fury* (1929) and *So Red the Rose* (1934), respectively. The 1940s brought works by James Street, Eudora Welty, and Richard Wright, and Faulkner received the Nobel Prize in 1949. Ellen Douglas's *A Family's Affairs* and Margaret Walker's *Jubilee* were published in the 1960s. Novelists Faulkner, Welty, Richard Ford, and Donna Tartt have won Pulitzer Prizes. Other prominent novelists include Larry Brown, Ellen Gilchrist, John Grisham, Barry Hannah, Thomas Harris, Greg Iles, Willie Morris, Walker Percy, and Elizabeth Spencer. In 2011, Jesmyn Ward won the National Book Award for *Salvage the Bones*.

Columbus native Thomas "Tennessee" Williams launched his career in 1945 with *The Glass Menagerie* and his 1947 play, *A Streetcar Named Desire*. In 1955 his *Cat on a Hot Tin Roof* won the Pulitzer Prize. Pulitzer Prize winners in journalism include Hodding Carter, Ira Harkey, William Raspberry, and Hazel Brannon Smith. Many others achieved distinction in nonfiction, poetry, and drama, including authors Will D. Campbell, David H. Donald, William Ferris, Shelby Foote, Anne Moody, and James Silver; poets Beth Ann Fennelly, William Alexander Percy, Sterling Plumpp, and Al Young; Pulitzer Prize–winner and nineteenth Poet Laureate of the United States Natasha Trethewey; and Pulitzer Prize–winning playwright Beth Henley.

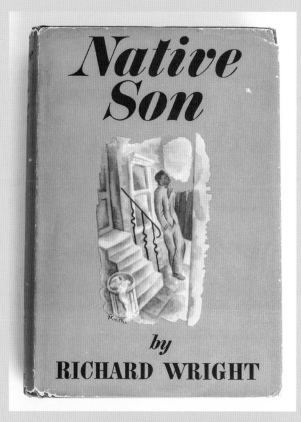

Native Son, novel, by Richard Wright, ca. 1940. Wright was born on a plantation outside of Natchez and grew up in Jackson before moving to Memphis, then Chicago, New York, and Paris. His work relayed the struggles of African Americans in the early twentieth century.

Royal R700 typewriter, manufactured in 1971. Eudora Welty typed the majority of her fiction on a series of Royal manual typewriters. She switched to electric typewriters in the late 1970s when arthritis made it too difficult to continue using her manual. This was the last manual typewriter owned by the author.

CONTRIBUTIONS TO TELEVISION AND FILM

Many native Mississippians have worked in television and film since each medium's inception, from silent film actress Martha Mattox to Academy Award–winning actor Morgan Freeman. Other actors and actresses from Mississippi include Gerald McRaney, Evelyn Preer, Beah Richards, Tonea Stewart, and Sela Ward. Jerry Clower entertained many as a comedian. Journalist Robin Roberts and talk show host turned media mogul Oprah Winfrey are both native Mississippians. Robert Pittman of Jackson founded MTV, and Robert L. Johnson of Hickory founded BET. Leland native Jim Henson created the Muppets, including Kermit the Frog, who first appeared on *Sesame Street* in 1969. Henson provided the voice and movement for Kermit and dozens of other Muppets on television and film until his death in 1990.

INTERNATIONAL BALLET COMPETITION

Ballet educator Thalia Mara secured Jackson as the location of the first International Ballet Competition held in the United States. Produced in 1979, the USA IBC was recognized by UNESCO, joining three other rotating host countries. Every four years, the competition brings gifted dancers to Jackson for two weeks of elite performances.

MISSISSIPPI CIVIL RIGHTS MUSEUM

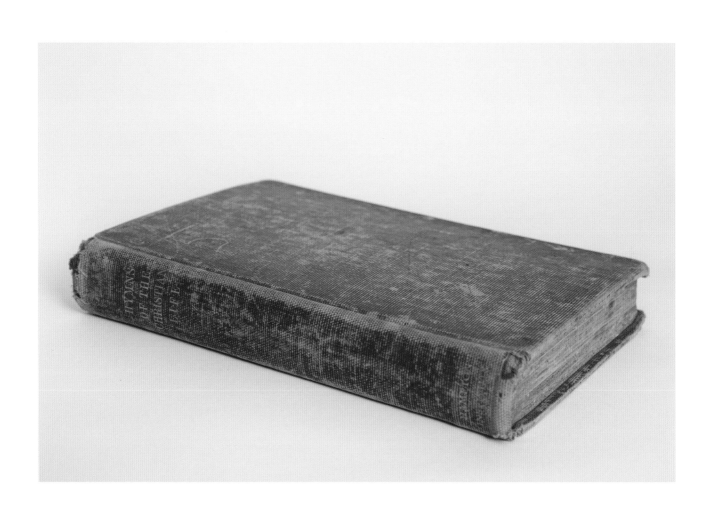

Introduction

JOHN E. FLEMING, PHD

T HE GREATEST GENERATION is a term made popular by the journalist Tom Brokaw in describing the men and women who survived the Great Depression and went on to make the world safe for democracy. I, likewise, use the term to describe the remarkable African American men and women, born during the height of the Jim Crow era, who decided to take a stand against injustice that changed a nation. This is a story about what it means to be an American and the struggle to attain the American Dream.

The concept of liberty and freedom are embodied in our founding documents—the Declaration of Independence and the United States Constitution. Our founding fathers had declared their willingness to die for their freedom, while enslaving Africans and their descendants. It is within this context that Mississippi became a state in 1817. Because America was a nation whose foundation was based upon the institution of slavery, Mississippi was not an anomaly in American history. This notion of freedom and justice for all that permeated American history did finally give rise to Emancipation, citizenship, and the right to vote for African Americans during the Reconstruction era. However short-lived the Reconstruction experience was, these founding principles of liberty and freedom would inspire the modern-day Civil Rights Movement.

Our primary goal in developing this exhibition was to tell the truth. The exhibition does not shy away from the unspeakable horrors of the Jim Crow era and the atrocities that were committed in the name of preserving white privilege. The exhibition tells the stories of individuals with indomitable spirit who not only survived these horrendous acts of violence, but also emerged triumphant in their search for freedom and the American Dream.

Hymns of the Christian Life, clothbound book, published by A. S. Barnes & Co., 1925. This hymnal first belonged to William Henry Holtzclaw Jr., whose father William Henry Holtzclaw, founded the Utica Normal and Industrial Institute in 1903 to educate black children. A. M. E. Logan later owned the hymnal. Logan was active in the Civil Rights Movement, founding Womanpower Unlimited to assist Freedom Riders and their families.

The Mississippi Civil Rights Museum is composed of artifacts, documents, art, images, and stories. Combined, these elements form a narrative that reveals the struggle of a generation of men, women, boys, and girls who took a stand in the name of freedom. That struggle ultimately led to the emancipation of both black and white Mississippians. We begin our story within the black communities from which the movement would eventually emerge. Through personal stories, we relate how difficult it was for individuals to take a moral position against injustice in a closed society, and we unabashedly tell how the courage to act often resulted in a high cost for them and their families.

We refrain from moralizing; we allow the participants and their actions to speak for themselves. We witness Fannie Lou Hamer's eloquent speech before the Democratic National Convention in which she said, "If the Mississippi Freedom Democratic Party is not seated now, I question America." We focus on lesser-known women such as Mrs. Willie Mae Cotton, who operated a freedom house in McComb. We neither indict nor judge members of the KKK and the white Citizens' Council. The records are there in the files of the Sovereignty Commission. They are also recorded in local newspapers that did not shy away from reporting on the brutal murders of men and women who dared to exercise their right to vote.

Traditionally, men have been at the forefront of social movements. While men may have appeared at the head of various Civil Rights groups, in reality it was the women, and later young people, who were the backbone of the Movement. Young people gave the Movement momentum even in the face of increased violence. They were the catalyst that created the "tremor in the iceberg." Their courage empowered entire communities throughout the state—Greenwood, Natchez, Port Gibson, and many others.

For those of us who participated in and lived through the Movement, the Mississippi Civil Rights Museum offers an opportunity to relive and learn from that very horrendous experience. For some, it may be catharsis; others may wish to pay homage to those who suffered that all may be free. We hope that by visiting the museum, people will learn from individuals who made a difference by taking a stand against injustice, that they can change a nation as well.

This exhibition will stir our emotions. But only by calling up these tragedies and sufferings from our shared past can we begin the process of racial reconciliation. It is through the recognition of these atrocities that we can begin the process of learning from our failures and move forward to improve our communities, our state, and our nation.

We ask our visitors to reflect on our founding documents in which our civil and human rights are embedded. History matters! How we remember and interpret history is essential to understanding who we are today and how we came to be Mississippians and Americans. This exhibition offers the state of Mississippi an opportunity to reconsider its collective memory that is marred by racism, bigotry, and the notion of white supremacy. This exhibition allows all of us to harness a realistic collective memory that strengthens our efforts to ensure that social justice exists for current and future generations.

We take seriously the American Alliance of Museums' call for museums to go beyond merely collecting and preserving artifacts to serving as educational institutions. Thus we fully recognize our obligation to promote social justice for all. It is not by chance that the visitor continuously goes through the gallery "This Little Light of Mine." It is here that visitors can see how individual acts of courage can change society. It is through these acts of courage that Mississippi today is a better society. That is the legacy that Civil Rights workers left to the State of Mississippi and that is the legacy that the Mississippi Civil Rights Museum leaves to the people of Mississippi as we celebrate the founding of this state 200 years ago. It is here that we consecrate, commemorate, and celebrate our collective memory as we move through the twenty-first century.

Mississippi's Freedom Struggle

THE MISSISSIPPI CIVIL RIGHTS MOVEMENT represents a heroic chapter in the centuries-long African American freedom struggle. Men, women, and children from every corner of the state risked their lives to mount a courageous campaign to win their civil rights. They sued for freedom in the courts. They sought freedom in the vote. They demanded freedom in the press. They marched for freedom in the streets. History shows us that American democracy is imperfect. The Mississippi freedom struggle reminds us that every person has a light, and in a democracy, that light has the power to propel us all forward.

HUMAN CARGO AND PROFITS

From 1502 to 1839, European and American traders shipped some twelve million enslaved Africans across the Atlantic. New World colonists grew wealthy using slave labor to harvest timber, work mines, and grow tobacco, sugarcane, and other crops. By 1776 southern landowners had grown dependent on slavery. They refused to sign the Declaration of Independence until a passage condemning slavery was removed.

In Mississippi, slavery predates statehood. French rule brought Caribbean Creoles as slaves to Biloxi in 1721, British rule brought Jamaican-born African Caribbeans to Natchez, and Spain offered land grant bonuses to settlers willing to bring slaves. In the 1790s high cotton prices and new technology like the cotton gin triggered a rush of American settlers to fertile Mississippi. As cotton production soared, so too did the demand for slave labor. On December 10, 1817, Mississippi entered the Union as a slave state.

86 Lashes to Go **from the** *Slave* **series,** cotton, quilt by Gwendolyn A. Magee, ca. 2004. In 1823 Mississippi passed its own code governing "slaves, free negroes, and mulattoes." The code restricted slave movements and activities while protecting masters' property rights. Slave punishments included lashes on the bare back, burned hands, maiming, and death.
© The Estate of Gwendolyn A. Magee, Artist.

One Hundred Negroes for Sale

BY THE FIRST OF NOVEMBER, we will be at the "Forks of the Road," near Natchez, with 100 NEGROES for sale. They are all young, have been carefully selected, and consist of

FIELD HANDS,
HOUSE SERVANTS,
AND MECHANICS.

☞ We will be in receipt of fresh lots every few days during the season.

BLACKWELL, MURPHY & FERGUSON.

oct80—d;w tf —

☞ N. O. Picayune and Delta insert the above two months, and send bill to this office for collection.

Advertisement for slave sales, Natchez *Daily Courier,* November 27, 1858. Forks of the Road, Natchez.

Slave pen key, brass, early to mid-nineteenth century.

Forks of the Road—Natchez Slave Market

Traders sold enslaved people at Aberdeen, Crystal Springs, Vicksburg, Woodville, and Jackson, but the Natchez Forks of the Road slave market was by far the most active. At peak times, the market's 500 slaves gave it the look of a sprawling prison camp. Traders shipped slaves by steamboat or caravans, called "coffles," with mounted guards, driving slaves down the Natchez Trace. The market stayed open until 1863, when Union troops occupied Natchez.

A NATION DIVIDED OVER SLAVERY

In 1787 framers of the Constitution argued over how to count enslaved people in determining representation and taxation. The North, with fewer than 50,000 slaves, did not want to award congressional seats to southerners based on a population that included about 650,000 slaves. Southerners objected to being taxed on population and property. The resulting compromise counted slaves as "three-fifths" of a person. This slavery-inflated number of seats gave southern congressmen power and influence in Washington.

North along the Underground Railroad

"We hold these truths to be self-evident, that all men are created equal, that they are endowed by their Creator with certain unalienable Rights . . ." The Declaration of Independence, while having no legal standing, became a moral force that inspired free and enslaved blacks during the struggle for freedom and motivated northern abolitionists to campaign to outlaw slavery. From 1810 to 1850, about 100,000 runaways found freedom along the Underground Railroad. Fellow slaves helped most reach the North, where they received aid from free blacks and white abolitionists. By 1863 about 70,000 runaways had found freedom in Canada.

Tipping toward War

Passions over slavery, both for and against, grew with the nation. In 1820 Congress adopted the Missouri Compromise—any free state would be admitted if balanced by the admission of a slave state. The compromise held until the Kansas-Nebraska Act of 1854 left the issue of slavery up to the residents of each territory. Three years later, Dred Scott sued for his freedom, but the Supreme Court ruled that as a black man, Scott could not be a citizen and could not bring suit. The Court ruled that Congress had no authority to regulate slavery in the territories. The country tipped toward war.

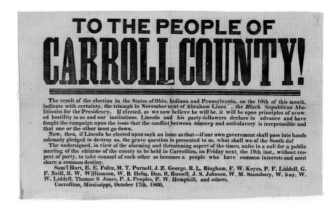

Call to People of Carroll County broadside, October 17, 1860. Southerners viewed the election of Abraham Lincoln and the Republican Party as a threat to slavery.

Mississippi, the South's leading cotton producer, joined the Confederacy in February 1861. The South tried to withhold cotton to draw England into the war as an ally, but surplus stores kept England neutral. Some 80,000 white Mississippians fought for the South. Seventeen thousand black Mississippians joined the Union army, serving with the United States Colored Troops.

Congress Outlaws Slavery

Congress outlawed slavery by passing the Thirteenth Amendment on January 31, 1865, following intense lobbying by President Lincoln. Three years later, the Fourteenth Amendment granted African Americans equal protection under the law. Southern states were required to ratify this amendment to gain representation in Congress. For the first time, all citizens were counted to determine the number of seats each state would receive in the House of Representatives. However, with the solidification of Jim Crow laws and black disfranchisement in the coming decades, white southern politicians once again gained undue power in Congress.

Pay Sheet for August & September 1866

Name	Time	Rate per day	Full Amt	Pd Amt	Cotton
William Wills X	4-3/4	5-7/2	25.20		lbs
Sidney Wills X	39-3/4	27-1/2	17.54		660 " 40¢ per wt settle
Barber Wilkinson	30-1/2	57-1/2	17.70 X		lbs
Louisa Wilkinson	22-1/4	41-2/3	10.08 X		205 " "
Amelia Wilkinson	41-1/4	16-2/3	6.87 X		
Henderson Cole	47-1/4	50	23.62 X		
Cilla Cole	41-1/4	33-1/3	13.75 X		
George Cole	41-1/2	50	21.37 X		155 " lbs
Elizabeth Cole	33-1/2	33-1/3	12.64 X		220 "
Charles Helm	29-3/4	57-1/2	18.61 X		365 "
Jane Helm	35-1/2	41-2/3	16.33 X		385 "
Ben Helm	39	46	18.62 X		160 "
Milly Helm	33	41-2/3	14.89 X		285 "
Isham May	41	57-1/2	23.62 X		
Violet May	42-1/2	41-2/3	17.70 X		
Milly May	23-1/2	16-2/3	3.90 X		
Maria Mon	35-1/4	41-2/3	15.88 X		300 "
Mayhala Goins	19-1/4	12-1/2	2.40 X		
Jim Crow	41	57-1/2	24.64 X		255 "
Eliza Crow	44-1/4	37-1/2	16.35 X		220 "
Becky Morrison	35-1/2	41-2/3	14.79 X		
Becky Thomas	25-3/4	12-1/2	3.21 X		
Tom Rivers	34-3/4	53-3/4	18.70 X		
Mandy Chase	23-3/4	37-1/2	8.90 X		
John Williams	37	57-1/2	23.72 X		600 "
Lucinda Brown	38-1/4	37-1/2	15.92 X		395 "
John Calhoun	34-3/4	26-3/4	9.70 X		90 "
A.C. Calhoun	39-3/4	33-1/3	14.35 X		275 "
Harriet Calhoun	34-1/4	33-1/3	12.55 X		305 "
			$433.44		

21 Acct Paid in full

witness Wm B Lewis

his
Isham May
mark

Mississippi in Black and White

B EFORE THE CIVIL WAR, black Mississippians had lived in enslavement for more than a century. After the war, the Thirteenth Amendment outlawed slavery. The United States Army enforced a federal policy called Reconstruction, intended to rebuild the southern states and bring them back into the Union.

Blacks emerged from slavery with their first hopeful glimpses of freedom. They eagerly built communities with businesses, schools, and churches. They voted and won election to office. But black freedom was fragile, guarded by the northern army. Mississippi whites resented northern troops and northern land speculators. They had grown up treating blacks as property. They did not relish sharing the state's wealth and political power with people they viewed as inferior. When Union army occupation ended, so too did enforcement of blacks' civil rights.

EMERGING FROM SLAVERY: RECONSTRUCTION

During Presidential Reconstruction under President Andrew Johnson, the daunting task of rebuilding homes, farms, and communities began. Black "freedmen" sought their own land. White legislators sought to solidify white rule and keep black workers on the plantation. In November 1865 they passed new Black Codes and other laws restricting the movement of freed people.

To counter such moves, Congress called for Congressional or "Radical" Reconstruction, dismantling President Johnson's plan. In 1867 General Edward Ord ordered the registration of all eligible voters, who would elect constitutional convention delegates. Most whites refused to participate, hoping to deny the election the majority required to call a constitutional convention.

Cotton worker pay sheet, 1866. No longer slaves, black Mississippians entered into labor contracts, often with their former masters.

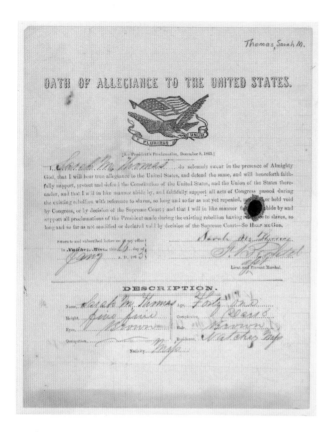

Loyalty oath, signed by Sarah M. Thomas of Natchez, January 16, 1865.

When their plan failed, they found themselves a minority in state government.

From 1867 to 1869, Mississippians elected thirteen black state senators and 102 representatives. In the 1870s Alexander K. Davis served as lieutenant governor, Rev. James D. Lynch and James Hill as secretaries of state, and John Roy Lynch and Isaac D. Shadd as speakers of the state house. At a time when US senators were elected by state legislators, Mississippi sent Hiram Rhodes Revels and Blanche Kelso Bruce to Washington. John Roy Lynch became a member of the House. However, whites continued to hold most local and county offices. Blacks never gained a majority in the state legislature despite comprising 54 percent of the population in 1870.

Writing a New State Constitution

Mississippi rejoined the Union and held elections for federal offices by passing its 1868 Constitution and ratifying the Fourteenth and Fifteenth Amendments. Convention delegates included seventy-nine Republicans and seventeen conservatives; blacks claimed eighteen seats. Northern newcomers, derisively called "carpetbaggers" by former Confederates, held twenty-three seats. The 1868 State Constitution allowed "all male inhabitants" to vote. Former Confederates had to sign loyalty oaths to receive amnesty from the president.

FLOWERING BLACK COMMUNITIES

Black communities grew from the ashes of the Civil War. In Jackson, Biloxi, Vicksburg, and elsewhere, separate black neighborhoods, business districts, schools, and churches developed. In 1910 land ownership among blacks peaked nationally at fifteen million acres—nearly every Mississippi county had a few landowning black farmers. Black professionals, tradesmen, and merchants succeeded in Mississippi cities by serving black customers.

Denied education as slaves, free blacks sought schools for their children. White opposition and the absence of public schools in many rural areas created obstacles. Black churches often doubled as schools, or ran schools. Northern foundations such as the Rosenwald Fund gave "matching" money to build black schools. Following elementary school, some black students received industrial training at Piney Woods, Prentiss, and Utica. Colleges in Jackson, Alcorn, and Tougaloo offered rare chances for higher education.

Mound Bayou, the Jewel of the Delta

After the Civil War, railroad companies coming to the Delta offered large tracts of land at low prices and would then purchase the timber new landowners had cleared. Seizing the opportunity, Isaiah T. Montgomery and Benjamin T. Green led a group of blacks to settle Mound Bayou, which became known as "the Negro capital" and "the Jewel of the Delta." By 1907 some 800 families (4,000 people) made their homes in and around the colony. The town expanded to include a sawmill, thirteen stores, six churches, three cotton gins, a bank, telephone exchange, and weekly newspaper, the *Demonstrator*.

Mound Bayou boomed from 1890 until World War I, when it entered several decades of decline. In 1912 the colony became financially overextended over the construction of the Mound Bayou Oil Mill and Manufacturing Company, which failed in 1915. Its decline shook a local economy already struggling to survive low cotton prices, the boll weevil's arrival in 1908, the 1912–13 floods, and stiff competition from local white planters.

Banner from Stringer Lodge, F. & A.M., No. 1, silk lined with cotton, late nineteenth century. The Reverend Dr. Thomas W. Stringer incorporated Mississippi's first black Masonic lodge in Vicksburg on December 27, 1867.

ISAIAH MONTGOMERY,
Founder of Mound Bayou, Servant of Jefferson Davis
(See Page 159.)

Isaiah T. Montgomery, engraving from
Alexander's Magazine, 1907. Montgomery
founded the town of Mound Bayou with his
cousin, Benjamin Titus Green, in 1887.

Choppers . . . And Johnny, photograph by
Leigh Briscoe Allen, early twentieth century.
John Wesley Fairley was a former slave who
owned land in Stone County and supervised
white men in the logging industry.

KING COTTON'S SYSTEM OF CHEAP LABOR

Cotton was king—the international commodity had helped the Union recover from the costs of the Civil War. The state's largest industry succeeded
primarily by employing workers at low cost. Over time, floods, the boll weevil,
and years of low cotton prices forced small farmers, especially black farmers,
out of business until what remained were mostly large plantations owned by
white planters. Behind "King Cotton," white Delta planters became rich and
powerful, influencing both state and national politics.

White legislators in control after 1875 passed laws meant to secure white
supremacy while solving the labor shortage. The "Pig Law" made the theft
of an animal worth more than ten dollars punishable by up to five years in
prison, while the Leasing Act allowed the state to lease convicts out if their
sentences were less than ten years. Together, the laws permitted a system in
which blacks could be arrested, sentenced to prison, and leased out to private interests. The 1890 Constitution replaced the convict lease system with

a system of state prisons. Parchman Penitentiary, set on 20,000 acres and modeled on the plantation system, later became the icon of that system.

The sharecropping system also provided cheap labor to plantation owners, who contracted with multiple tenants. These sharecroppers—black and white—were provided land and shelter in return for a "share" of the cotton profits. The system favored planters, who prospered while sharecroppers struggled. Most large plantations operated a store where tenants could buy food and supplies on credit. In many cases, sharecroppers were paid in tokens that could only be used at the plantation. Exploitation was rampant as planters kept the books and took advantage of farmers, many of whom were illiterate. In disagreements over payment, blacks had nowhere to turn. Few sharecroppers could work enough land to climb out of debt, and this poverty was passed down through generations.

Parchman Penal Farm—male prisoners hoeing in a field, photograph, date unknown. Convicts worked cotton fields, extracted turpentine gum, built railroads, and worked on any number of public and private projects.

JIM CROW RULES AND IMPOSING A SYSTEM OF WHITE SUPREMACY

Congress abandoned Reconstruction before the process was complete, leaving Mississippi's government and its black citizens vulnerable to white supremacists. The First Mississippi Plan in 1875 assigned voter registration to local white registrars and redrew legislative districts to favor whites. Voter intimidation and fraud became commonplace, causing the black vote to drop off dramatically—at least 66 percent did not or could not vote in the 1880 presidential election.

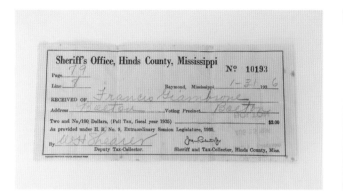

Poll tax receipt, 1936. State law required payment of the two-dollar poll tax to vote. It disproportionately affected poor people, most of whom were black.

"Colored" sign, mid-twentieth century. "Colored" and "White" signs marked entrances to public spaces and segregated amenities like restrooms and water fountains. This sign marked the entrance to a Greenville doctor's office.

The new legislators began to systematically deprive blacks of their civil rights. In 1888 the first Jim Crow laws began to reinforce segregation as social custom, dictating where blacks could ride, walk, eat, work, play, and go to school. The Second Mississippi Plan came in 1890. The new state constitution used literacy tests and poll taxes to effectively bar blacks from voting. Fewer than 10 percent of blacks managed to qualify in the next two Mississippi elections. Other southern states modeled their constitutions on the Mississippi document.

The Great Migration

For many black Mississippians, the only way to escape Jim Crow, especially violence and economic hardship, was to leave the state. Between 1910 and 1960, nearly a million people fled to northern cities. They were drawn by the promise of higher-paying jobs, better schools, and some degree of social equality.

In 1890 blacks made up nearly 60 percent of Mississippi's population and just under 10 percent of all blacks in America. By World War II, for the first time in more than a century, the state's population was over 50 percent white. Despite the migration, more than a million blacks remained in Mississippi, still proportionately more (49.2 percent in 1940) than in any other state.

ABANDONED BY THE LAW

With little fear of arrest or punishment, whites employed violence or its threat to maintain supremacy. From 1877 to 1950, Mississippi accounted for 600 lynchings, nearly 13 percent of the black men and women lynched nationwide. Twenty-four reported lynching victims after 1888 were white, and fifteen were women. Blacks could be lynched, as Holly Springs native Ida B. Wells-Barnett wrote, "for anything or nothing." In particular, romance between a black man and a white woman was fiercely punished.

Black leaders around the country called for federal laws to ban lynching. In the 1890s the Afro-American League and the National Equal Rights Council led the anti-lynching movement. Ida B. Wells-Barnett published numerous pamphlets documenting the injustice of lynching. In 1917, after white-led race riots in his home district of East St. Louis, US Representative Leonidas C. Dyer introduced a bill in the House to outlaw lynchings. The bill passed overwhelmingly, but southern Democrats killed it in the Senate with a filibuster. Similar bills failed to pass in the 1930s.

Rise of the Ku Klux Klan

The Klan represented the most vicious side of Jim Crow. During Reconstruction, they threatened black voters and sympathetic whites, but their activities were curbed by Union troops. When the troops left, the Klan became bolder, carrying out night-rider attacks against black churches, teachers, and schools. In 1870 Congress passed the Enforcement Act, which allowed perpetrators to be tried in federal rather than local courts, but white juries consistently refused to render guilty verdicts against Klan members. After 1871 night-rider activities waned as the state pursued legal mechanisms to rob blacks of the vote. The Klan experienced a rebirth following World War I. While many disapproved of its "bedsheet violence," by 1925 the Klan counted 8.9 million members, 93,000 in Mississippi.

Klan robe and hood, cotton, found in a Jackson home, ca. 1910–1915.

Local people and friends march in Hattiesburg, four days after the death of Dr. Martin Luther King Jr., photograph by Winfred Moncrief, April 8, 1968.

THIS LITTLE LIGHT OF MINE

POINTS OF LIGHT—LOCAL PEOPLE AND FRIENDS WHO CAME TO HELP

The power in any democracy lives within its people. When they fail to act, democracy languishes. When people rise and act, great things are possible. In the Mississippi Civil Rights Movement local people—rich and poor, male and female, young and old—from every corner of Mississippi stepped forward, often at great personal risk, to demand equal treatment and equal opportunity under the law. The cause of freedom also drew brave, generous, and talented people of all races from all over the United States. Some had personal ties to family and friends in Mississippi. Some saw it as a moral calling to help those in need. Others viewed their freedom and the freedom of all Mississippians as one—where one person or group of people are threatened by injustice, all are at risk. The following entries honor just a few of the people who propelled the Movement forward.

Rev. James D. Lynch

A native of Baltimore, Rev. James D. Lynch served as a missionary for the A.M.E. Church in South Carolina and Georgia during the Civil War, helping establish black schools and churches. In 1868 he brought his work to Mississippi. Lynch became one of the founders of Mississippi's Republican Party and served as its first vice president. In 1869 he won election as Mississippi secretary of state, the first African American to hold that office.

We're gonna light a lamp in Ruleville, and it's gonna shine all over that Delta.
—CHARLES MCLAURIN, OXFORD, OHIO, JUNE 1964

John Roy Lynch, carte de visite, ca. 1870s.

Rep. John Roy Lynch

The child of a slave mother and Irish plantation manager father in Vidalia, Louisiana, John Roy Lynch was sold with his mother to a Natchez planter after his father's death. A self-educated man, Lynch operated a photography studio and became active in the Republican Party after the war. Governor Adelbert Ames appointed him justice of the peace in 1869. That same year, he won election to the state legislature, later serving as Speaker of the House. In 1873 he won election to the US House of Representatives, serving three terms.

Sen. Blanche Kelso Bruce

Born a slave in Virginia, Blanche Kelso Bruce left his master at the beginning of the Civil War and moved to Hannibal, Missouri, where he taught school briefly before continuing his education at Oberlin College in Ohio. After the war, Bruce worked on a Mississippi steamer for a year before settling in Bolivar County, where he became a successful planter. Bruce served as sheriff and tax collector before the state legislature elected him to the US Senate. He was the first African American senator to serve a full term, from 1875 to 1881.

Sen. Hiram R. Revels

An ordained minister who was born free in North Carolina, Hiram Revels followed the Union army to Jackson, where he lectured and organized black churches and schools. Moving to Vicksburg in 1864, he served as chaplain of a black regiment and minister of the Bethel A.M.E. Church. In 1866 Revels became pastor at Zion Chapel A.M.E. Church in Natchez. There, he was appointed alderman before winning a seat in the state senate in 1869. A year later his colleagues elected him the first African American US senator.

Dr. T. R. M. Howard

Dr. T. R. M. Howard came to Mound Bayou in the 1940s to serve as chief surgeon at the Knights and Daughters of Tabor Hospital. He also owned a plantation and the Magnolia Mutual Insurance Company. In 1951 Dr. Howard founded the Regional Council of Negro Leadership in Cleveland, which called for "first class citizenship for Negroes in Mississippi." His rallies drew thousands, hosting national figures like Thurgood Marshall and Mahalia Jackson.

Ida B. Wells-Barnett

A Holly Springs native, Ida B. Wells-Barnett attended Shaw University (today's Rust College) before moving to Memphis to teach. She was arrested in 1884 for refusing to give up her seat on a railroad car. Wells-Barnett sued and won the case, but the ruling was overturned on appeal. In 1892 three of her friends were lynched. When she denounced the killings in the newspaper *Free Speech and Headlight* and called for a boycott of white businesses, the newspaper office was burned, and Wells-Barnett was warned to leave town. She moved to New York then Chicago, where she became a leading voice in the anti-lynching campaign and the women's suffrage movement.

Richard Wright

The son of a Natchez sharecropper and a high school teacher, Richard Wright grew up in Roxie and Jackson before moving to Chicago in the 1920s. As a writer, he gave voice to the experience of American racism, including his own encounters, which he described in *Black Boy* (1945): "My life as a Negro in America had led me to feel . . . that the problem of human unity was more important than bread, more important than physical living itself; for I felt that without a common bond uniting men . . . there could be no living worthy of being called human."

Dr. T. R. M. Howard, photograph, ca. 1950s.

The human family might be of many colors, but they're still human, and they possess the personality, the image, the likeness of God, in many ways. So, it is my hope that we can live together and work together . . . and try to accomplish something in the period of time we've got.

—Amzie Moore, Cleveland, Mississippi, 1977

Ida B. Wells-Barnett, journalist and civil rights activist, photograph by Oscar B. Willis, date unknown. Photographs and Prints Division, Schomburg Center for Research in Black Culture, The New York Public Library, Astor, Lenox and Tilden Foundations.

Hazel Brannon Smith

In 1964 Hazel Brannon Smith earned a Pulitzer Prize for her reporting on race, but she paid a heavy price. Editor/owner of the *Lexington Advertiser*, Smith wrote that all races "should have the same protection of the laws and courts." She condemned the Citizens' Council "Gestapo" tactics, called for the disbanding of the Sovereignty Commission, and criticized the police attack on Tougaloo Nine supporters. Smith hosted activists and printed their materials. In 1964 her Jackson newspaper office was bombed. Saddled with huge debts caused by a boycott, she was forced to declare bankruptcy.

Pulitzer Prize for Distinguished Editorial Writing, awarded to Hazel Brannon Smith, May 4, 1964.

Rabbi Perry Nussbaum

A Toronto native, Rabbi Perry Nussbaum came to Jackson's Beth Israel Congregation in 1954. In 1961 Nussbaum was moved by the sacrifices of the young Freedom Riders, about a third of whom were Jewish. He tried to organize the state's rabbis to visit them at Parchman, but none agreed. So, each week he drove north to Sunflower County to deliver personal items and cigarettes, and he led a short worship service for both Jews and non-Jews. Back in Jackson, he wrote to their families.

Ella Baker

Veteran community organizer Ella Baker guided the evolution of the Student Nonviolent Coordinating Committee (SNCC) at Shaw University in North Carolina in April 1960. She encouraged students to look beyond the "hamburger" politics of lunch counter sit-ins. She challenged them to connect people's personal troubles to larger social issues and to reach out to women and youth. Baker helped SNCC flourish by mentoring Bob Moses, Diane Nash, Julian Bond, and other student leaders.

The measure of freedom has now been heard in every part of
Mississippi because you took it there.

—Bob Moses, Freedom Vote victory celebration, 1963

Brenda Travis

In 1961, at age fifteen, Burglund High School student Brenda Travis spent weeks
canvassing her McComb neighbors for voter registration. She lied about her age
to join the Greyhound terminal sit-in, where she and fellow student Ike Lewis
were arrested for breach of the peace. Following their release, the high school
principal refused to admit them back into school. Travis led the resulting walkout
of 116 students to city hall, where they were arrested. Travis was expelled and
sentenced to the Oakley reformatory school. In 2006 Burglund High gave hon-
orary degrees to those who had been expelled. Randall O'Brien, who had been
a twelve-year-old boy in McComb during the walkout, presented Travis with the
bronze star he had earned in Vietnam, saying, "Thank you, Brenda, for who you
are and for who you've helped me to become."

Father Nathaniel

A native of Detroit, in 1950 Father Nathaniel Machesky came to Greenwood,
where he established the St. Francis of Assisi Mission to aid the poor. St. Francis
offered religious services and education. When local banks refused loans to
blacks, Father Nathaniel established the St. Francis Federal Credit Union. During
the Greenwood Movement, Father Nathaniel made his facility available for food
distribution, alienating some white supporters.

Dr. James W. Silver

In his book *Mississippi: The Closed Society*, history professor James W. Silver wrote
about the 1962 riot following James Meredith's admission to the University of
Mississippi and the culture of oppression in the state. He wrote, "When the
state of Mississippi was being flooded from within by malignant propaganda

about what had happened at Ole Miss that fateful night, I felt a growing compulsion to try to tell the truth." For his efforts, Silver was called "the most hated white man in Mississippi." Silver remained until 1965, when he took leave to teach at the University of Notre Dame. He never returned.

Eudora Welty

Jackson native Eudora Welty was a writer of international acclaim whose novels and short stories earned numerous literary awards, including the 1973 Pulitzer Prize for her novel *The Optimist's Daughter*. In "Where Is the Voice Coming From?" (1963), Welty wrote from the perspective of Medgar Evers's killer (then unknown). She said about the piece: "That hot [June] night when Medgar Evers . . . was shot down from behind in Jackson, I thought, with overwhelming directness: Whoever the murderer is, I know him: not his identity, but his coming about, in this time and place." The short story was published in the *New Yorker* less than one month after the murder.

Rev. Ed King

In 1963, at great personal risk, Vicksburg native Rev. Ed King agreed to run for lieutenant governor on the state's first integrated ticket since Reconstruction. He accepted the role reluctantly, still recovering from wounds suffered in a June car crash in which he and John Salter had been forced off the road. As Tougaloo College chaplain, King had joined Medgar Evers and Salter in the Jackson Movement. He and his wife, Jeannette, transported Tougaloo students to the March on Washington at a time when sharing a car with blacks put them at risk. King also worked to desegregate Jackson's white churches. For his activism, King became estranged from his parents and colleagues in the clergy.

Ed King, Miss. native supports racial integration, photograph by Matt Herron, November 14, 1963. Rev. Ed King with Myrlie Evers, widow of slain civil rights leader, Medgar Evers. © Matt Herron / Take Stock / The Image Works.

Anne Moody

Anne Moody's *Coming of Age in Mississippi* (1968) offered a firsthand account of her life as a young black woman in Mississippi. Moody picked cotton, went to segregated schools, and sang in church choirs. She was shaken by Emmett Till's murder and ongoing violence against her neighbors. Moody pursued higher education at Tougaloo, where she joined the Movement. She sat in at the Capitol Street Woolworth's, marched after the murder of Medgar Evers, and volunteered to staff CORE's Freedom House in Canton. Her memoir describes the difficult work required to recruit youths to the Movement and gain the trust of rural people, all while suffering harassment from local whites.

Margaret Walker and fellow poets: Naomi Long Magdett, Mari Evans, Sonia Sanchez, Margaret Walker, and June Jordan, photograph by Roy Lewis, 1973. Courtesy Margaret Walker Center, Jackson State University. © Roy Lewis Archives 1974.

Tracy Sugarman

Returning from World War II, illustrator Tracy Sugarman felt "the mounting urgency of the racial crisis." He volunteered for the 1964 Summer Project, where he worked on voter registration in Ruleville and became friends with Fannie Lou Hamer. His Freedom Summer sketches appeared in various magazines and the CBS news documentary *How Beautiful on the Mountains*. In 1966 Sugarman published *Stranger at the Gates*, a memoir of his experiences.

Florence Mars

At the University of Mississippi in the 1940s, Florence Mars and classmate Betty Pearson spoke out for black laundry workers. In 1954 they were shocked by the Emmett Till trial, where Mars took numerous photographs. In 1964 Mars was running a Neshoba County stockyard and teaching Sunday school. She initially found it hard to believe that local Klansmen had killed three young civil rights workers (James Chaney, Andrew Goodman, and Michael Schwerner), but when her questions led Mars to the truth, she took the information to FBI investigators. For her role, neighbors boycotted her business, and Mars was forced to sell.

Margaret Walker

An English professor at Jackson State College from 1949 to 1979, Dr. Margaret Walker Alexander inspired blacks to learn their own history and determine their own future. In 1937 Walker had published her breakthrough poem, "For My People," which portrayed the pain of blacks' daily lives while celebrating their strength. In 1966 Walker published her signature novel *Jubilee*, which tells the African American story from slavery through the Civil War and Reconstruction. In 1968 Walker founded the Institute for the Study of History, Life, and Culture of Black People (now the Margaret Walker Center) at Jackson State, where she served as director.

State Representative Robert Clark

Robert Clark of Holmes County was the first African American elected to the Mississippi Legislature in the twentieth century. A public high school teacher and coach, Clark served as project director of the Migrant Farmer's Education Program and was a member of the county Community Action Program board. In the 1967 election, Clark defeated twelve-year state House veteran J. P. Love by just 116 votes in a single-member district. He went on to serve thirty-six years in the legislature, where he was chairman of the House Education Committee. For twelve years, he served as Speaker Pro Tempore.

US Congressman Walter E. Fauntroy and Representative Robert Clark confer in Jackson, photograph, ca. 1980s.

Fannie Lou Hamer

A native of Montgomery County, Mississippi, Fannie Lou Hamer was instrumental in organizing Freedom Summer, fought tirelessly for voting rights, and cofounded the Mississippi Freedom Democratic Party. In her nationally televised testimony to the Credentials Committee at the 1964 Democratic National Convention, she spoke passionately about her own experiences with discrimination in Mississippi. Hamer said, "If the Freedom Democratic Party is not seated now, I question America." Hamer challenged party leaders to uphold America's commitment to equality under the law. With fellow congressional candidates Annie Devine and Victoria Gray, she took the challenge to Washington, DC, in January 1965. She continued to speak for civil rights and to advocate for poor people until her death in 1977.

Fannie Lou Hamer singing to a group of people during the March Against Fear through Mississippi, begun by James Meredith, photograph by Jim Peppler, June 1966. Alabama Department of Archives and History, Montgomery, Alabama.

WE SING FOR FREEDOM

Freedom's voice came to Mississippi in song. People sang for courage. They sang for unity and strength. They sang for inspiration and joy. They sang to nourish hope. In cottonfields and country churches, at county courthouses and county jails, in freedom schools and on college campuses, they sang. We shall overcome. Ain't gonna let nobody turn me around. We shall not be moved. Fannie Lou Hamer is often associated with the song "This Little Light of Mine." The song and Hamer's life remind us that the power of any democracy lives within its people.

"Everyone gathered in a circle, crossed arms, joined hands, and swayed out the many powerful verses: 'We are not afraid. . . . Truth shall set us free. . . . God is on our side. . . . We shall overcome.' A powerful effect was felt by all as we sang freedom songs. . . . The music often brought individuals and the community through difficult times."
—Sue Sojourner, Holmes County

"I began to see the music itself as an important organizing tool . . . not only to bring them together but also as the organizational glue to hold them together."
—Sam Block

"The spiritual was like an explosion to me, an emotional explosion. . . . The music and the religion provided a contact between our logic and our feelings . . . and gave the logic of what we were doing emotional and human power to make us go forward."
—Jean Wheeler Smith

"I well remember singing it. . . . It speaks to our heritage of slavery and oppression, as well as of our hope for equality, freedom, and justice."

—Gwendolyn A. Magee

Lift Every Voice and Sing, cotton, velvet, satin, and leather, quilt by Gwendolyn A. Magee, 2004. © The Estate of Gwendolyn A. Magee, Artist.

A Closed Society

As they had done in World War I and earlier conflicts, black Mississippians served in America's armed forces and worked in homefront industries during World War II. But increasingly they asked, "Where is our freedom?" Black newspapers displayed a bold "Double V"—victory abroad and victory at home. Black soldiers and nurses returned to Mississippi with new perspective, having seen the world beyond the segregated South. They came home to a state transformed by war, but still holding fast to Jim Crow. As the war in Europe and Asia wound down, the battle lines at home were drawn.

WAR COMES TO MISSISSIPPI

World War II homefront industries and military camps jump-started Mississippi's economy. At the same time, the number of farms shrank while farm sizes swelled. Sharecroppers and farm tenants were displaced by chemical weed killers and cotton-picking machines, allowing landowners to consolidate vast tracts. Some of those workers enlisted in the military, while others sought jobs in wartime industries, despite widespread racial discrimination.

Mississippi cities bustled with industrial and construction workers—who were mostly white—and more than a million men and women were stationed at thirty-six military bases across the state. Movement of people to new places, along with stress caused by the war, increased racial tensions, especially in cities that were located near the segregated bases, such as Centreville, Hattiesburg, and Grenada. Many soldiers came from outside the South and were unfamiliar with Jim Crow customs, leaving them vulnerable to white brutality.

Change of Classes Parade, photograph by Mark Lenihan, date unknown. Biloxi's Keesler Air Force Base opened in June 1941 as a training center for pilots and aviators. Thousands of students marched twice daily in the "change of classes" parade.

Black Mississippians Go to War

More than 85,000 black men and women from Mississippi served in the US armed services during World War II. They were initially excluded from the Marines and the Army Air Corps. The army put them in segregated units and assigned them to the supply services, where they worked in maintenance and supply transport. The navy assigned them as messmen. Black women served in the Women's Army Corps (WAC) as nurses, restricted to stations with black hospitals until 1944.

As war needs became more pressing, roles expanded. Black soldiers in the 761st Tank Battalion landed on Omaha Beach, Normandy, on October 10, 1944. Many black soldiers, including Medgar Evers, operated the Red Ball Express, a truck convoy that supplied Allied forces as they rolled across Europe. The all-black 332nd Fighter Group, the Tuskegee "Red Tails" (a moniker derived from their aircrafts' painted tails), escorted Allied bombers over Europe. From 1941 to 1946, nearly a thousand black pilots flew some 15,500 combat sorties and earned more than 150 Distinguished Flying Crosses.

Tuskegee Red Tails, oil on canvas, by Clenard Martin, 2013. This painting depicts five Tuskegee pilots escorting a bomber: Col. Benjamin O. Davis Jr. (#66), Lt. Quitman C. Walker of Indianola, MS (#A-4-3), Lt. John F. Biggs (#30), Lt. Carl B. Carey (#46), and Lt. Roy M. Spencer (#77).

THE BEGINNINGS OF A MOVEMENT

Black veterans were determined to challenge Jim Crow. Many joined the National Association for the Advancement of Colored People (NAACP) and the Regional Council of Negro Leadership. Nationally, the NAACP grew from 50,556 members in 335 branches in 1940 to over 500,000 members and in 1946 more than a thousand branches. In 1944 NAACP branch director Ella Baker reported 129 members in six branches in Mississippi. Largely middle class, the NAACP pursued a methodical legal strategy—bring suit in court to challenge existing state laws and customs, then test the court decisions once given. They pressed for voter registration, anti-lynching laws, and ending discrimination in housing, education, and employment.

The Effects of Brown v. Board of Education

In May 1954 the Supreme Court's decision in *Brown v. Board of Education* determined that segregation in schools was unconstitutional. The ruling sent shock waves throughout the South, stirring passions in both the black and white communities. White southerners pledged to maintain segregation in the name of states' rights while blacks harnessed newfound optimism to continue the fight for equality.

In July 1954 white supremacists created the Citizens' Council in Indianola and formed groups throughout the South. Two years later, Citizens' Councils claimed 80,000 members in sixty-five counties. Members influenced elections,

NAACP pennant, felt, 1963. This pennant belonged to the Evers family. Medgar Evers served as Mississippi field secretary for the NAACP from 1954 to 1963.

Citizens' Council sign, metal, used in Jackson, MS, 1960s.

Emmett Till murder trial, photograph by Florence Mars, September 1955. Reporters swarmed officials outside the Tallahatchie County Courthouse in Sumner during the Emmett Till trial.

promoted segregation, and attacked the *Brown* decision through all forms of printed and broadcast media.

The NAACP also saw a surge in membership. The group urged black parents to petition local school boards to demand integration. Local white officials threw out the petitions, and black parents had their names published in the newspaper, making them targets of Citizens' Council members.

On March 29, 1956, the Mississippi Legislature created a new state agency, the Mississippi State Sovereignty Commission, to "protect the sovereignty of the state of Mississippi, and her sister states" from "encroachment thereon by the Federal Government or any branch, department or agency thereof." Until 1973 the commission promoted segregation in Mississippi and investigated its perceived enemies. The commission files are today accessible via the Mississippi Department of Archives and History's website.

The Murder of Emmett Till

In August 1955 Emmett Till, a fourteen-year-old Chicago native visiting relatives in the Mississippi Delta, was murdered and thrown in the Tallahatchie River for reportedly whistling at a white woman in a grocery store. Stricken over the loss of her son, Mamie Bradley insisted on an open casket so everyone could see what had happened to him. *Jet* magazine and the *Chicago Defender* published photos of the mutilated body.

The trial put Mississippi under a scorching spotlight as journalists from around the world descended on the Sumner courthouse. Till's uncle, Moses Wright, identified Roy Bryant and J. W. Milam as the men who abducted Emmett Till, but a jury of white men took only sixty-seven minutes to find them not guilty. FBI research later revealed that jury members had been visited by the Citizens' Council to ensure they voted "the right way." The verdict provoked outrage. Black youths identified with Till, and many later described it as the moment that led them into the Movement.

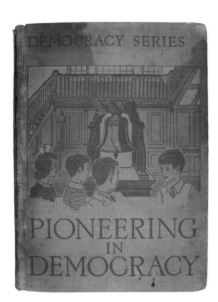

Pioneering in Democracy, textbook, 1942. This textbook was used at Mississippi Negro Training School in Jackson.

THE BATTLE OVER SEGREGATION BEGINS

Speaking for a unanimous Court, in regard to the *Brown v. Board of Education* case, Chief Justice Earl Warren stated, "separate facilities are inherently unequal.... Segregation is a denial of equal protection of the laws."

Mississippi's white officials, who did not agree with the Court's decision, considered three responses to the verdict: flagrantly defy the Court, close public schools in favor of private schools, or spend millions to improve black schools, in return asking black leaders to support "voluntary segregation." In July 1954 Governor Hugh White chose the third option. After floating his plan with a few sympathetic educators and ministers, Governor White invited ninety black leaders to meet in Jackson. On July 30 the tense meeting resulted in attendees formally denouncing voluntary segregation.

By World War II, no state spent less on black students than Mississippi. Black children made up 57 percent of the school population but received only 13 percent of the funds for public schools. In 1940 a quarter of the state's eighty-two counties had no black high school, and the black school term was only six months.

VIOLENCE AGAINST THE MOVEMENT

Violence and economic intimidation by white supremacists left the Movement stumbling in the late 1950s. Key leaders were targeted. In May 1955, two weeks after a rally of 10,000 blacks in Mound Bayou, Rev. George Lee was shot to death while driving along a Belzoni street. In August, Lamar Smith was gunned down in broad daylight outside the Brookhaven courthouse. In November, Gus Courts was fired upon in his own store. Courts recovered, but he fled the state.

Black voter registration and NAACP membership dropped sharply because of Citizens' Council intimidation and white violence. NAACP regional field secretary Ruby Hurley had reported 52,364 members in 349 branches in 1955. By 1957, she counted just 221 branches with 26,775 members.

Medgar Evers: The NAACP's Man in the Field

Medgar Evers reflected the passion of World War II veterans determined to challenge Jim Crow. He used the GI Bill to earn a degree from Alcorn State. After graduation, Dr. T. R. M. Howard hired Evers to work as an agent for the Magnolia Mutual Insurance Company in Mound Bayou, where he also attended political rallies at Howard's plantation. As an agent traveling the state, Evers saw black poverty and hopelessness firsthand. In 1954 Evers was denied admission to the University of Mississippi law school.

His actions brought him to the attention of the NAACP, which hired Evers as the first fulltime state field secretary in December 1954. He organized local chapters across the state, recruited members, and set up youth councils. Evers also investigated, documented, and publicized violence and illegal discrimination against blacks, often calling for federal intervention. He worked on well-known cases, like the Emmett Till case, and dozens of lesser-known incidents. For his activism, Evers received many death threats.

Myrlie and Medgar Evers in their Mound Bayou home, photograph, ca. 1950s. Medgar and Myrlie Evers met as students at Alcorn and married in 1951. Evers's activism was motivated by his deep love for his wife and three children, whom he wanted to grow up in a society that was free from racism and injustice. Courtesy of Mrs. Myrlie Evers.

NATIONAL ASSOCIATION FOR THE ADVANCEMENT OF COLORED PEOPLE

TWENTY WEST FORTIETH STREET • NEW YORK 18, N. Y. • LOngacre 3-6890

Please direct reply to:
Mr. Medgar W. Evers
1072 Lynch Street, Room 7
Jackson 3, Mississippi

FLeetwood 3-6906

October 18, 1960

Dr. Gilbert Mason
742 Nixon Street, Apt J
Biloxi, Mississippi

Dear Dr. Mason:

Relative to our conversation the last time
I was in your city of Biloxi, I have written the en-
closed letter to the persons whose names appear thereon. I am anxious to get something going here in Jackson to the point that I am willing to risk even life
itself.

We have procrastinated long enough in the state
and the trestment from the whites has not lessened rather
increased. My feeling is, if we are to receive a beating,
lets receive it because we have done something, not because we have done nothing. Let me hear from you on this
right away.

Sincerely yours,

Medgar W. Evers
Field Secretary

MWE:11
Encls

A Tremor in the Iceberg

I N THE EARLY 1960s, a new generation of activists rose to breathe fresh urgency into the Civil Rights Movement. World War II veterans had emphasized voter registration and legal challenges in the courts. This younger generation seemed more determined to confront Mississippi segregationists directly and publicly.

Sit-ins, Freedom Rides, and sidewalk pickets would shake Mississippi and draw the eyes of the nation. From a Pike County jail, activist Bob Moses described it as the "tremor in the middle of the iceberg." Young activists came from Mississippi and beyond its borders, providing energy, new methods, and courage, perhaps steeled by their naiveté about the waiting consequences. Older people provided experience, contacts, and material support.

MISSISSIPPI SIT-INS

The Sit-in Movement succeeded through public, nonviolent confrontation. The Congress of Racial Equality (CORE) and the Student Nonviolent Coordinating Committee (SNCC) recruited students to participate. Newspaper photos and television broadcasts showed peaceful black protesters being attacked by white mobs or bullied by police, which highlighted the injustice and put pressure on the president and Congress to act. Mississippians launched sit-ins in Biloxi, Jackson, Greenville, and Clarksdale.

The concept of the sit-in inspired similar forms of protest. Dr. Gilbert Mason spearheaded the Biloxi wade-ins at public beaches in April 1960, while Tougaloo College students in Jackson staged a read-in at the public library in March 1961. About 1,500 blacks rallied in solidarity following the arrest of

Letter from Medgar Evers to Dr. Gilbert Mason, October 18, 1960. Evers advised his friend Mason, a local physician and founding president of the Biloxi branch of the NAACP. Mason teamed with Gulfport NAACP president Dr. Felix Dunn to organize the Harrison County Civic Action Committee. Courtesy of the National Association for the Advancement of Colored People.

Razor, metal, made by Gillette, ca. 1963. NAACP leaders Medgar Evers and Gilbert Mason collaborated on civil rights activities until Evers's death. Medgar Evers left this razor during an overnight visit to Dr. Mason's house on the Sunday before his death. Evers quickly left the Mason home in Biloxi after receiving a phone call that he was needed in Jackson.

Police arrest Tougaloo students sitting in at the Jackson Public Library, still image from WLBT newsfilm, March 27, 1961.

the "Tougaloo Nine." Myrlie Evers later described it as "the change of tide in Mississippi." Medgar Evers had worked on all of these demonstrations.

On April 7, 1961, Mississippi NAACP president Aaron Henry and other state leaders met with NAACP executive secretary Roy Wilkins and his staff in New York. They agreed to launch "Operation Mississippi," a direct action campaign intended to encourage black students to desegregate public places. As a result, Jackson students sat in at both local bus terminals, a Walgreen's lunch counter, Jackson's Livingston Park and public zoo, and local swimming pools. In Greenville, NAACP youth council members picketed downtown chain stores. Vicksburg students picketed a movie theater. Clarksdale students were arrested for trying to buy train tickets at the "white window."

HERE COME THE FREEDOM RIDERS

James Farmer and CORE recruited young people, black and white, to participate in an integrated bus ride on May 4, 1961, from Washington to New Orleans. They intended to integrate bus station waiting rooms, lunch counters, and public restrooms, testing enforcement of a recent Supreme Court decision that outlawed segregation in interstate travel. The Freedom Riders expected

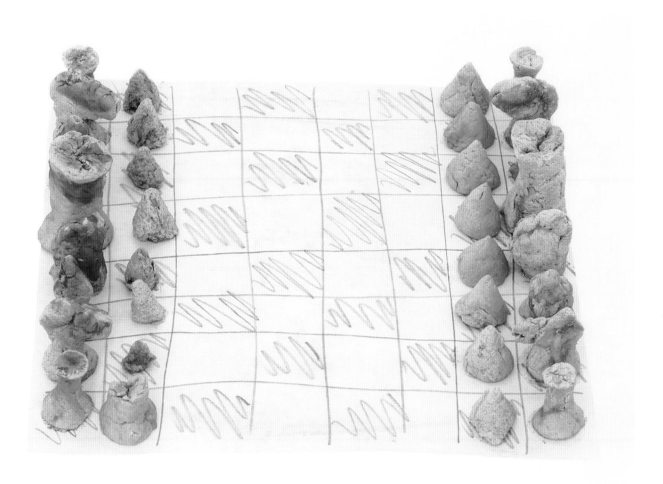

to provoke opposition that would compel the federal government to enforce the law, but the resulting violence surprised even CORE. After a calm trip to Atlanta, they were mobbed, beaten, and their bus firebombed in Alabama.

To avoid further bloodshed (and bad publicity), US Attorney General Robert Kennedy worked out a plan with Mississippi senator James Eastland: if police would guarantee the safety of the Freedom Riders, the federal ruling on interstate travel would not be enforced. Upon arrival at Jackson's Trailways terminal, Freedom Riders exited the bus and went inside—blacks

Chess set, bread and paper, by Freedom Rider Carol Silver at Parchman, 1961. "I . . . used about six slices to mold a set of chess pieces. By wetting the bread with spit, we could mold it much like the plasticine clay I remember having as a child. . . . Then came the problem of coloring them to make one set black, and, of course, Joe suggested using blood." Courtesy of Tougaloo College Archives, Carol Ruth Silver Collection.

Flip flops, plastic, 1961. Freedom Rider Joan Trumpauer (Mulholland) received these sandals from Womanpower Unlimited while she was imprisoned at the Hinds County jail. Womanpower founder Clarie Collins Harvey teamed with Jesse Mosley, Aurelia Young, A. M. E. Logan, and other Jackson women to help Freedom Riders and their families. After the Freedom Rides, Womanpower supported ongoing voter registration campaigns and anti-segregation boycotts.

entered the white waiting area; whites entered the "colored" section. When they refused police orders to move on, they were arrested and charged with "breach of the peace." Unwilling to pay the $200 fine, Freedom Riders were sentenced to sixty days in jail and sent to Parchman penitentiary, where they risked physical harm or worse. Activists kept in regular contact with John Doar and the Justice Department. The NAACP hired local attorneys to provide counsel. The Riders bonded at Parchman, emerging as folk heroes and hardened Movement activists.

GRASS ROOTS EFFORTS AND THE BIRTH OF COFO

Southern Christian Leadership Conference (SCLC) volunteer Bob Moses came to the Delta in 1960 to recruit activists for SNCC's fall conference. In Cleveland, he met Amzie Moore, a postal worker, businessman, and vice president of the state NAACP. Their collaboration produced a community-based voter education campaign that began in 1961. In McComb, Hattiesburg, Jackson, and other cities, young organizers partnered with community leaders. Local people provided credibility, contacts, housing, and office space. As part of the Council of Federated Organizations (COFO), they educated black citizens and promoted voter registration, though they faced stiff, violent opposition.

COFO gave black Mississippians a civil rights organization that spoke for them. It emerged from a working group put together by NAACP state president Aaron Henry to meet with Governor Ross Barnett in 1961. A year later, Henry and Medgar Evers met with leaders of SNCC and CORE to establish the umbrella organization. COFO united the NAACP, SNCC, CORE, SCLC, and other groups to coordinate activities and share funding.

While men dominated the governing positions of civil rights organizations, women made up the majority of the ground troops. Women served as movement planners, field organizers, clerical staff, youth counselors, fund-raisers, and political candidates. They hosted activists in their homes. They canvassed neighbors and filled mass meeting halls. They picketed courthouses, distributed food and clothing to the poor, and taught citizenship classes. And while women may have appeared less threatening to the white establishment, they went to jail and suffered violence alongside their male colleagues.

Voter Registration Campaigns

McComb was the first site for the new voter registration campaign. Amzie Moore sent Bob Moses to work with local NAACP president C. C. Bryant in 1961. Moses spoke at churches and organized youth councils, tapping into NAACP work done by Medgar Evers. By the end of August, SNCC had sent a dozen activists, and they broadened their reach to Walthall and Amite Counties.

Activists Hollis Watkins and Curtis Hayes began SNCC's voter registration campaign in Forrest County in March 1962, working with local people like Vernon F. Dahmer Sr. Mrs. L. E. Woods provided COFO office space on the first floor of her hotel. After a half-dozen people were unsuccessful in their attempt to register, the team formed the Forrest County Voters League, and by September 100 blacks had attempted to register. Only four succeeded. Victoria Gray became project director and hosted adult literacy and citizenship classes.

SNCC moved into the Delta in 1962, setting up an office in Greenwood. Activists reached out to poor folks in Ruleville, Indianola, and Cleveland. Greenwood became a battleground, however, following the February 28, 1963, highway shooting of SNCC staffer Jimmie Travis. SNCC, CORE, SCLC, and the NAACP all brought in more staff to support their efforts. President John F. Kennedy's administration sent John Doar and a team of FBI agents. On March 30 a federal lawsuit was filed against the city, which called for the release of jailed activists and the end of interference with voter registration. The resulting compromise released the jailed organizers, but little else changed.

"I am Mrs. Vera Pigee, a wife, a mother, political prisoner, business and professional woman. Wherever I go, even if I am brought in handcuffs, my name is still Mrs. Vera Pigee."

—Vera Pigee, Clarksdale activist

Boycotting Clarksdale's White Businesses

"If we can't PARADE downtown, should we TRADE downtown?" was the question asked by Clarksdale's black community in November 1961, when local black marching bands were excluded from the holiday parade. Aaron Henry suggested a boycott—since 70 percent of the county residents were black, a boycott would have real teeth, and local people could participate with less risk. With Henry's leadership, members from the NAACP, SNCC, CORE, and the SCLC cooperated without the rivalries that had distracted movements elsewhere. In 1962 the boycott goals expanded to include downtown employment above the menial level, the use of courtesy titles, voting rights, school desegregation, the integration of public facilities, and the formation of a biracial committee. In April 1962 Martin Luther King Jr. spoke to a thousand local people, urging them to "stand in, sit in, and walk in by the thousands."

The Jackson Movement

The Jackson Movement featured crippling boycotts of downtown merchants and the state fair. Medgar Evers became the face of this movement and, increasingly, the target of death threats by those who opposed it.

"Black Christmas" reached Jackson in December 1962 as students and community leaders boycotted downtown merchants. They demanded courtesy titles, equality in employment, and an end to Jim Crow practices. Demands also included the hiring of black police and crossing guards and the formation of a biracial committee to review race relations. Mayor Allen Thompson rejected the demands.

On May 28, 1963, Tougaloo students and faculty sat in at the downtown Woolworth's lunch counter. They were assaulted by a mob of white Jackson Central High students and were escorted out by police. The scene, shown on the local news, inspired other boycotts. On May 31, police arrested some 450 demonstrators—many high school students—marching downtown and chanting, "We want freedom!" National NAACP leaders urged compromise, partly due to mounting bail costs, now at $64,000. The Jackson Movement lost momentum.

CRISIS IN THE DELTA

SNCC workers asked, "What good is it to desegregate a lunch counter if you have no money for food?" Poor families, many of whom lost jobs with the modernization of cotton production, relied on the federal commodity relief program to obtain basic foodstuffs. However, in 1962, after SNCC's voter registration campaign, the Leflore County Board of Supervisors voted to discontinue the program for people not on welfare. Sunflower County restricted eligibility as well. Some 22,000 people—about 90 percent black—had to look elsewhere for assistance.

SNCC put out a national call for help, and friends in the North responded. Musician Harry Belafonte hosted a benefit at Carnegie Hall. Comedian Dick Gregory chartered a plane and flew tons of food to the Delta. Michigan State students Ivanhoe Donaldson and Ben Taylor drove a truck loaded with donated supplies to Clarksdale during Christmas break. SNCC organized food distribution centers. Fannie Lou Hamer saw their work

NEGRO SHOPPERS AND FRIENDS!

The Jackson Movement Belongs To YOU

It Is Strong and Powerful—
Supported By Many, Many **THOUSANDS**
Picketing, Leaflet Distribution, Church Visits, Mailing of Literature, and Mass Meetings Will Continue - - -
Until We ALL Win: 1. EQUALITY in Hiring and Promotion
2. END of Segregated Drinking Fountains - Restrooms - Seating
3. Use of COURTESY TITLES: "MRS.", "MISS" & "MR."
4. SERVICE on a FIRST-COME, FIRST-SERVED basis.
STAND UP For Dignity and Freedom!
DON'T BUY ON CAPITOL STREET
(State St. To Mill St.) or at the following other businesses, wherever they may be located in JACKSON:
Hall-Holmes (Bagby Hall), Jitney Jungle grocery stores, McRae's dept. stores, Wilkinsons 555 tire & appliance stores, and STAR ("Luck-Super") Groceries.
Tell Your Friends to Support the Movement!
WIN FREEDOM FOR ALL!
❖ **JACKSON MOVEMENT** ❖

Flier for Jackson Movement boycott, ca. 1962–1963. Tougaloo students handed out fliers in black neighborhoods and picketed Capitol Street in downtown Jackson to promote the boycott.

Tear gas canister and grenade, recovered after the riot at Ole Miss, 1962. Trying to fend off the angry mob, federal marshals shot tear gas, littering the grounds in front of the Lyceum with the empty canisters.

as a turning point: "Nobody never come out into the country and talked to real farmers. . . . If you hadn't arrived at a certain level, you wasn't treated no better by blacks than you was by the whites. And it was these kids what broke a lot of this down."

RIOT AT OLE MISS

James Meredith's attempt to register at the University of Mississippi triggered a bloody riot outside the administration building on September 30, 1962, making national headlines. Students and white supremacists from Mississippi and elsewhere surrounded the Lyceum, where federal marshals were reportedly guarding Meredith. Violence escalated in the night with bottles and bricks being thrown, fires set, and gunfire. The marshals fired tear gas to try to disperse the crowd. Ole Miss professor James Silver and Rev. Duncan Gray made appeals to the crowd with little success. President Kennedy ordered in National Guard and regular army troops from Memphis.

The violence took the lives of two people, French journalist Paul Guihard and white Oxford bystander Ray Gunter, both killed by gunshots. Federal marshals suffered 160 injuries, including twenty-eight gunshot wounds. At dawn, some 23,000 soldiers stood guard over campus. That same morning, protected by armed soldiers, James Meredith registered and attended his first class. Federal marshals escorted him during his entire year on campus.

MEDGAR EVERS IS ASSASSINATED

Medgar Evers was shot in the back by sniper Byron de la Beckwith outside his Jackson home just after midnight on June 12, 1963. He later died at the hospital. The shooting came hours after President Kennedy announced on national television that he would send sweeping civil rights legislation to Congress. Evers left behind his wife, Myrlie, and children Darrell, Reena, and James Van Dyke Evers. His funeral in Jackson drew some 4,500 people, including national

civil rights leaders Ralph Abernathy, Roy Wilkins, and Dr. Martin Luther King Jr. With Jackson police out in force, the funeral march nearly exploded into a full-scale race riot as black youths expressed their outrage. Like the murder of Emmett Till, Evers's death provoked deep sorrow and fierce outrage. Evers was buried in Arlington National Cemetery. President Kennedy met with Myrlie, Darrell, and Reena Evers at the White House, signing a draft copy of the civil rights bill that was signed into law in 1964.

1917 Enfield .30-06-caliber rifle, wood and metal, ca. 1917. Police found this rifle, owned by Byron de la Beckwith, in the bushes across the street from the Evers home. Beckwith went free after two mistrials in 1964. In 1994 he was convicted for Evers's murder and sentenced to life in prison.

IN THE UNITED STATES DISTRICT COURT FOR
THE SOUTHERN DISTRICT OF MISSISSIPPI
JACKSON DIVISION

- - - - - - - - - - - - - - - - - X

BETTE POOLE, et al.,   :

                         Plaintiffs, :

              - against -   :   AFFIDAVIT

ROSS R. BARNETT, etc., et al.,   :

                         Defendants. :

- - - - - - - - - - - - - - - - - X

STATE OF MISSISSIPPI   )
                       : ss.:
COUNTY OF   )

        BETTE POOLE, being duly sworn, deposes and says:

        I am one of the plaintiffs herein. I make this af-

fidavit in support of the complaint herein, the request for

interlocutory relief and the request for a temporary restrain-

ing order.

        I am 19 years old and am a citizen of the United States

and a resident of the State of Mississippi. I am a student at

Tougaloo Southern Christian College. The other plaintiffs in

this action are Ida Hannah and Julie Zaugg. Miss Hannah is 19

years old and Miss Zaugg is 21 years old. Both are citizens

of the United States, students at Tougaloo Southern Christian

College and residents of the State of Mississippi. Miss Hannah

and myself are members of the Negro race and Miss Zaugg is a

Caucasian.

        On Sunday, October 6, 1963, we left the campus of

Tougaloo about 10:30 A.M. to drive into the City of Jackson in

order to attend Christian worship services at the Capitol Street

Methodist Church. We knew that Sunday, October 6, was World

Wide Communion Service at the Methodist Church.

I Question America

BY 1964 BLACK MISSISSIPPIANS were focused on freedom more than ever: Freedom Days, Freedom Democrats, Freedom Schools, Freedom Summer. Local movements had matured in 1963 and grown into a coordinated statewide campaign. Youths and seniors, middle class and poor, gathered in churches, Masonic halls, and community centers. They sang freedom songs outside county courthouses. They cast their ballots in a "Freedom Vote" and went to the Democratic National Convention to demand to be counted.

Most white Mississippians saw these activities, especially the 1964 Summer Project, as an invasion of "agitators" and "Communists." As black voices of freedom rang louder, white determination to silence them grew more desperate and more violent. Churches that echoed with freedom songs were rocked by explosions. Activists who canvassed for voter registration were jailed, beaten, and killed. The violence in Mississippi drew the eyes of the nation, and both would be forever changed.

> If the Freedom Democratic Party is not seated now, I question America. Is this America, the land of the free and the home of the brave, where we have to sleep with our telephones off the hook because our lives be threatened daily, because we want to live as decent human beings in America?
> —FANNIE LOU HAMER, 1964 DEMOCRATIC NATIONAL CONVENTION

ORGANIZING MISSISSIPPI: COMMUNITY ALLIANCES

By 1963 Mississippi's fledgling community movements were maturing. The collaboration of older people, full-time civil rights organizers, and youths began to raise hopes. The Movement was now reaching blacks in more and more places. Activists organized across the state in churches, beauty parlors, pool halls, lodges, cafes—wherever people gathered to talk.

Movement organizers set up makeshift offices and produced meeting fliers and voter registration applications on borrowed mimeograph machines. They used WATS telephone lines to communicate between offices and track

Affidavit by Tougaloo College student Bette Poole, October 12, 1963. Poole described her arrest for attempting to integrate the Capitol Street Methodist Church in Jackson on October 6. Courtesy of Tougaloo College Archives, Tougaloo Nine.

Henry-King Freedom Vote political button,
1963. "With all of my complicated feelings I
still had to agree with Moses that a ticket with
two Mississippi natives, one black and one
white, was a grand symbol. And so I entered
politics."—Rev. Ed King, "Freedom Vote"

**Hattiesburg blacks cast their Freedom Vote
ballots at the Masonic Temple,** photograph by
Winfred Moncrief, October 29, 1963.

field staff. WATS lines allowed unlimited long-distance calls for a flat fee and
bypassed local operators, who often blocked calls. COFO staff found rented or
donated office space and living quarters at Freedom Houses located in black
neighborhoods and business districts.

The SCLC's Annelle Ponder organized citizenship classes in Greenwood
and Grenada. In Ruleville, CORE's Dave Dennis organized a Home Industry
Cooperative to help women earn income through crafts. Tougaloo students
engaged in pray-ins at local white churches and organized boycotts of segregated performances by national artists. The "First Fourteen" attempted to
register to vote in Lexington, inspiring the Holmes County Movement.

Despite the Movement's far reach and progress, the work remained dangerous. On June 9, 1963, SNCC workers were attacked on their way home
to Greenwood from an SCLC workshop. Fannie Lou Hamer, June Johnson,
Annelle Ponder, Euvester Simpson, Rosemary Freeman, James West, and
others were arrested and savagely beaten for trying to integrate a café at the
Winona bus depot.

FREEDOM VOTE

With black people barred from the general election, COFO began organizing a mock election in September 1963 as an educational tool, which would also serve as a strong statement to Mississippi and the federal government that blacks wanted to vote.

The Freedom Ballot campaign began with a statewide convention in Jackson on October 6. The convention platform called for racial justice, school desegregation, the right to vote, and an economic program to help farmers and factory workers that included farm loans, an increased federal minimum wage, and labor's right to organize. NAACP state president Aaron Henry ran as candidate for governor, and Tougaloo chaplain Rev. Ed King ran as lieutenant governor, making it the first integrated ticket in Mississippi since Reconstruction.

Some 83,000 black Mississippians voted November 2–4. Media coverage, when not dismissing the Freedom Vote, focused on the white student volunteers. Bob Moses remarked that the election made it clear that "the Negroes of Mississippi will not get the vote until the equivalent of an army is sent here." That "army" would arrive in the summer of 1964.

THE KKK REINVIGORATED

The perceived failure of the Citizens' Council to stem the tide, in addition to the "invasion" of northern activists, led to the rise of more violent groups like the Ku Klux Klan. In May 1964 the House Committee on Un-American Activities estimated the Klan's membership at 6,000 in thirty-four Mississippi counties. Strongholds were Laurel, Natchez, Vicksburg, McComb, and Neshoba County, but their activities ranged statewide. During the two-month period

Burned cross, wood, 1964. The Ku Klux Klan burned this cross at the Vaccarella home in McComb on the night of August 12, 1964. G. T. Vaccarella had refused to contribute to the Citizens' Council and had hired African Americans to work in his grocery store. In November his home and business were shot into, and five men were sentenced to one year in jail for the crime.

if you are arrested in Mississippi

Prepared by the
NAACP LEGAL DEFENSE AND
EDUCATIONAL FUND, INC.

10 Columbus Circle
New York City, N. Y. 10019
Area Code: 212 JU 6-8397

NAACP Legal Defense Fund brochure, ca. 1964. The possibility of arrest was real for Summer Project volunteers. At the training sessions in Oxford, Ohio, SNCC's Jim Forman had told them "that they could all be expected to be arrested, jailed, and beaten this summer, and, in many cases, shot at."

of the Summer Project, Mississippi experienced more Klan violence than at any time since Reconstruction—COFO's 1964 tally listed 450 incidents, which included at least three murders.

Ongoing violence slowly eroded white Mississippians' support and tolerance of the Klan, with some publicly condemning it. In McComb, which became known as the "bombing capital of the world" during this period, *Enterprise-Journal* editor Oliver Emmerich denounced the violence in his editorials. In November McComb civic leaders drafted a Statement of Principles, signed by 650 local whites, calling for "equal treatment under the law for all citizens" and an end to violence and police harassment.

"The sheriff said that it was a planted bomb. I've worked 11 years to buy a house, and then do you think I would plant a bomb underneath the house with my two children in there? That's the kind of cooperation we are getting."
—Aylene Quin, who traveled with McComb bombing victims Matti Dillon and Ora Bryant to Washington, DC, where they met with President Lyndon B. Johnson and Assistant Attorney General Burke Marshall

FREEDOM DAYS

Freedom Days transformed attempts to register voters into multi-day events. By raising the profile of voter registration campaigns, Movement activists hoped to attract more media—maximizing their visibility, putting more pressure on white registrars, and enhancing the security of those trying to register.

Starting in January 1964 and continuing through the spring, COFO organized Freedom Days in Hattiesburg, Canton, Greenwood, and other Mississippi cities. Ministers from the National Council of Churches were invited to picket outside each courthouse and serve as witnesses. Historian/observer Howard Zinn recognized that the pickets marked a turning point: "Something unprecedented was taking place in . . . Mississippi: a black and white line of demonstrators was picketing a public building, allowed to do so by police."

FREEDOM SUMMER

SNCC's Lawrence Guyot described the 1964 Summer Project as a natural extension of the fall Freedom Vote and spring Freedom Days. Freedom Summer became a massive commitment by COFO to challenge white supremacy. Volunteers organized voter education classes and registration campaigns in black communities throughout the state. Mass meetings, pickets, Freedom Schools and community centers, Freedom Day events, and hundreds of out-of-state volunteers highlighted the high-profile campaign. Activists saw it as another chance to prompt the federal government to enforce the law by focusing the national spotlight on Mississippi.

Freedom Summer Volunteers

About 736 college students from around the country applied for the Summer Project. Elite private universities contributed about 40 percent of the student volunteers. Women made up 41 percent of the applicants. Whites made up more than 90 percent of the applicants. While some blacks did apply, financial challenges and the fear of violence in Mississippi limited their numbers.

COFO tallied approximately 450 student volunteers by July 3 (the total number would rise to about 650). Training sessions held in the North and South focused on nonviolence, voter registration, and Mississippi history. Volunteers performed a variety of functions, including clerical work, voter registration, writing and distributing information, teaching at Freedom Schools, organizing demonstrations, and more direct activism. Most volunteers experiencing the rural South for the first time were perplexed by southern customs and shocked by the poverty. Many lived with black families and formed lasting friendships. Following Freedom Summer, a number of participants dedicated their lives to social and political activism on a national level, standing up for civil rights, women's rights, the environment, and peace.

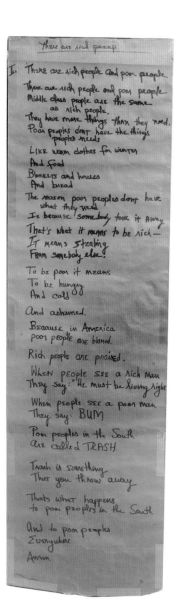

"There are rich people," handwritten poem, ca. 1964. This poem was written at a workshop held at the Highlander Folk School for Freedom Summer teachers and students.

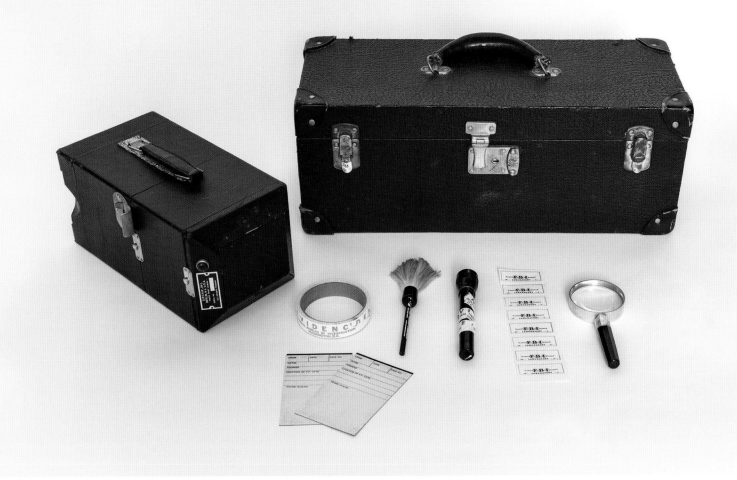

Chaney, Goodman, and Schwerner

At the beginning of Freedom Summer, CORE workers James Chaney and Michael Schwerner and summer volunteer Andrew Goodman were reported missing by their COFO colleagues. They had been arrested outside Philadelphia on June 21, 1964, and released, at which point the KKK pursued their vehicle, murdered them, and hid their bodies under an earthen dam. The disappearance of the three civil rights workers, and the ensuing Federal Bureau of Investigation (FBI) investigation, drew national attention and cast a long shadow of fear, remorse, and dread across the Summer Project.

Fingerprint camera and kit used by FBI field office, which opened in Jackson on July 10, 1964. By summer's end, the FBI had 153 agents working out of the Jackson office.

Freedom Schools and Community Centers

COFO developed Freedom Schools and community centers to strengthen community ties and build black self-esteem. SNCC field secretary Charlie Cobb first proposed the idea in 1963, after experiencing the poverty of the Delta, where black schools were underfunded, textbooks ignored black history, and curricula depicted blacks as inferior. Cobb thought the Movement ought to construct a parallel set of institutions "to fill an intellectual and creative vacuum in the lives of young Negro Mississippians."

Black Mississippians embraced the idea. Black churches and businesses offered meeting spaces. Parents and local residents donated supplies and labor to build community centers. State coordinator Staughton Lynd worked with educators and activists to develop a curriculum that emphasized maximum student participation and built on student experiences and knowledge. To classes in reading, writing, and mathematics, teachers added black history and the Civil Rights Movement. By summer's end, some 2,500 students (from preschool to high school) were attending nearly fifty schools around the state, more than double the original projection.

Poster, 1964. This poster urged the public to contact the FBI with information on the three missing civil rights workers. The remains of the young men were found on August 4. In 1967 seven men were convicted of conspiring to violate the men's civil rights. In 2005 Klan leader Edgar Ray Killen was sentence to sixty years in prison for the murders.

A FREEDOM DEMOCRATIC PARTY

Shut out of the all-white state Democratic Party, Movement activists formed the Mississippi Freedom Democratic Party (MFDP) on March 15, 1964, aiming to challenge the establishment at the national convention. On August 6 Ella Baker delivered the keynote address before some 2,500 statewide MFDP delegates at Jackson's Masonic Temple.

stand up for the FREEDOM DEMOCRATS

MFDP

Mississippi Freedom Democratic Party poster, ca. 1966–1967. Activist Rims Barber used this poster during voter registration drives.

The MFDP elected SNCC's Lawrence Guyot as party chair, Aaron Henry as delegation chair, and Fannie Lou Hamer as vice-chair. At the Democratic Party's national convention later that month, the MFDP challenged the seating of white delegates from Mississippi's Democratic Party.

In nationally televised hearings, the credentials committee heard stunning testimony from Hamer, Henry, and others. National party and civil rights leaders attempted to mediate the dispute. The resulting compromise—two at-large seats and honored guest status for the MFDP—left no one happy. Despite their enormous achievement, many returned home feeling disappointed, betrayed by the national leadership, and exhausted.

Black Empowerment

FREEDOM SUMMER and the challenge at the Democratic National Convention changed politics in Mississippi. Thousands of local people became engaged in the Movement. Their desire to claim their civil rights outweighed their fear of violence. Empowerment was taking hold in black communities. In rural towns, on college campuses, and in large cities, they began to march.

The next turning point, voting rights legislation, brought more opposition from hardline segregationists. When some Movement leaders left the state after years of dangerous struggle, local people picked up the torch. As is common in a democracy, they did not always speak with one voice. But a decade that began with Freedom Riders and sit-ins would end with black leaders taking seats in the state legislature.

TAKING IT TO THE STREETS

As the Movement matured, more black Mississippians took to the streets. In the late 1960s, marches in communities around the state demonstrated the unity and determination of blacks who overcame their fear of white violence and publicly demanded their civil rights.

They marched against fear from Memphis to Jackson. In Lexington they marched to register to vote. In Port Gibson they protested discrimination by downtown merchants. In Natchez they protested Klan violence. In Jackson they asked Congress to turn away Mississippians elected "illegally." In Marks they marched for poor people. They mourned the murder of a beloved local

leader in Hattiesburg and the shooting deaths of unarmed students at Jackson State College. In Grenada they escorted children to integrated public schools.

Marches drew the attention of police, white bystanders, and the media. Their visibility tended to prod federal, state, and local officials to respond to black grievances and work toward solutions.

March Against Fear

"Nothing can be more enslaving than fear," James Meredith told reporters on June 4, 1966, as he prepared to walk from Memphis to Jackson to encourage blacks to vote and overcome their fear of living and traveling in Mississippi. Just fourteen miles into his journey, Meredith was shot by Aubrey Norvell, a forty-year-old white hardware contractor. Meredith was treated for minor injuries and later returned to the march. The shooting turned the little-noticed march into a national event. By the time marchers reached Jackson on June 26, their numbers swelled to 15,000.

Port Gibson protesters march downtown to the courthouse, photograph by David Bethea, April 2, 1966. From 1966 to 1969, local people pursued voter registration and boycotted white Port Gibson businesses over a list of unmet grievances.

Four of Vernon Dahmer's sons, who returned from active duty to bury their father, overlook the ruins of the family home: George W. Dahmer, Sergeant 1st Class, US Army; Martinez A. Dahmer, Chief Master Sergeant, US Air Force; Vernon F. Dahmer Jr., Senior Master Sergeant, US Air Force; Alvin H. Dahmer, Specialist 4th Class, US Army, photograph by Chris McNair, 1966. A farmer and storeowner in the Kelly Settlement near Hattiesburg, Vernon F. Dahmer Sr. was a longtime voter registration activist and president of the Forrest County chapter of the NAACP. On January 10, 1966, the Klan firebombed his house and store, and Dahmer returned their fire so that his family could escape. His resulting death left the surrounding black and white communities outraged. © Chris McNair.

CHALLENGING MISSISSIPPI'S CONGRESSIONAL DELEGATION

In December 1964 the Mississippi Freedom Democratic Party (MFDP) filed a "notice of contest" to block the seating of five Mississippi congressmen victorious in elections that excluded blacks. Rep. William Ryan (D-NY) raised the motion when the House opened to seat new members on January 4, 1965. Ryan's "fairness resolution" was defeated 149–276. However, the three representatives being challenged directly by Fannie Lou Hamer, Annie Devine, and Victoria Gray were seated only provisionally pending a formal review.

Later that night, President Lyndon B. Johnson announced his Great Society agenda, a sweeping domestic program that included the Voting Rights Act and the so-called war on poverty. Afraid that supporting the challenge would jeopardize southern support for his agenda, Johnson maneuvered to delay the hearings until September. In the end, southern senators killed the challenge in committee. But in the meantime, the MFDP joined with about 150 volunteer attorneys to collect more than 600 depositions, documenting the systematic exclusion of blacks from Mississippi elections.

THE END OF COFO

In the wake of Freedom Summer, the Movement entered a transition. In 1965 key activists—chief among them Bob Moses and Dave Dennis—left Mississippi to finish school, pursue careers, and otherwise recover. Differences emerged over tactics and future plans, including whether whites should continue to be part of the Movement. Class distinctions fed rivalries—poor folks allied with SNCC and CORE, while the NAACP drew more middle-class blacks. At a COFO convention in Jackson, NAACP members complained about being drawn into COFO projects without having a say in planning. On March 7 the NAACP decided to pursue its own program for 1965. COFO was abolished in July. The Mississippi Freedom Democrats took over its projects.

MARTIN LUTHER KING IS ASSASSINATED

On April 4, 1968, Dr. Martin Luther King Jr. was shot by James Earl Ray outside the Lorraine Hotel in Memphis. Just weeks before his death, King had visited Greenwood and Marks to recruit volunteers for his Poor People's Campaign. In Greenwood he had preached to some 250 people at Jennings Temple C.M.E. Church and visited students at St. Francis Mission. Now, despite pleas for nonviolence, riots erupted in more than one hundred American cities. On April 5 President Johnson called for a national day of mourning.

More than a thousand people marched peacefully before heavily armed Mississippi National Guard troops in Greenwood. There was a similar march in Hattiesburg. Throughout Mississippi, blacks joined a weeklong boycott of white businesses. King's death jump-started the Greenwood Movement, renamed the "Greenwood Movement in Honor of Dr. Martin Luther King Jr."

STANDING UP TO VIOLENCE

The 1965 Voting Rights Act abolished literacy tests and sent federal officials to register voters and observe elections. As the law began to empower black voters, their calls for change grew louder. Nightly news broadcasts featured marches in Mississippi and across the nation. Fear was being replaced by pride and a willingness to fight back. At the same time, the Vietnam War was splintering the nation. Black youths questioned why they should fight to preserve freedom in South Vietnam when they could not exercise their civil rights in Mississippi.

Rifle, wood and metal with cotton strap, mid-twentieth century. While many people in the Movement practiced the philosophy of nonviolence, others took up arms in self-defense. This rifle was owned by Randolf "Rudy" Shields, a leader of the Port Gibson chapter of the Deacons for Defense. They guarded churches, homes, and businesses.

What Does Black Power Mean?

"Black Power" burst onto the scene during the 1966 March Against Fear. Released after his twenty-seventh arrest, SNCC leader Stokely Carmichael gave a passionate speech leading chants of "black power," a phrase SNCC had been trying out. Carmichael later described it as a political strategy—black people gain political control in areas where they make up the majority. Others interpreted the phrase in more militant or nationalist tones. The media reported it as a break from Martin Luther King's nonviolent stance. At the Jackson rally at the end of the March Against Fear, marchers announced their allegiance by chanting Carmichael's "Black Power" or King's "Freedom Now."

Law enforcement in riot gear on Lynch Street in Jackson, photograph, 1967.

Jackson State Shootings

Mounting anger over civil rights set the stage for deadly dramas on Lynch Street. A commuter corridor used by whites driving to and from Jackson's suburbs, Lynch Street cut through the Jackson State College campus. Whites were known to hurl racial slurs and objects at black pedestrians. Demonstrations occurred in 1963 following Medgar Evers's assassination and in 1964 when a motorist hit a JSC student. In 1967 bystander Ben Brown was killed by police gunfire on the second day of violence following police pursuit of a student who had been speeding.

The deadliest encounter occurred on May 14, 1970, the second night of conflict between law enforcement and black youths and just ten days after National Guard troops fired on students at Kent State in Ohio. Mississippi Highway Patrol officers and Jackson police opened fire on black youths at Alexander Hall, killing two young people—Phillip L. Gibbs (a JSC student)

Poor People's Corporation "dancing" doll, burlap and felt, 1965. Dr. Doris Derby worked for the Poor People's Corporation, where she helped develop the Liberty House Cooperative, which sold products like this doll.

and James Earl Green (a Jim Hill High School senior). Patrol officers claimed to have been responding to sniper fire, a claim refuted by witnesses and for which no evidence existed.

Mayor Russell Davis formed a biracial investigative committee that included black attorneys Reuben Anderson and Fred Banks. A majority found that what occurred was a "police riot." Federal and Hinds County grand juries refused to indict the officers.

Republic of New Africa

Formed in 1968, the Provisional Government for the Republic of New Africa (PGRNA) called on the United States government to grant $400 billion in reparations for slavery and racial oppression and to cede five southern states to form an autonomous black nation. They opened "consulates" in cities around the country. Brothers Gaidi Obadele and Imari Abubakari Obadele identified Mississippi's Black Belt as the "Kush District," where they might organize black independence through economic cooperatives, education, health care, militant self-defense, and respect for international law.

State and federal law officers closely monitored the group, and in the predawn hours of August 18, 1971, sixty FBI agents and Jackson police officers raided the PGRNA's Jackson headquarters. The ensuing gun battle killed Jackson police officer Lt. William Skinner and wounded a second officer and an FBI agent. After twenty minutes, seven PGRNA nationalists surrendered. At a separate Jackson residence, police arrested Gaidi Obadele and three other black nationalists. All of the "RNA 11" were tried for murder; eight received life sentences.

MISSISSIPPI'S WAR ON POVERTY

The needs of poor people had become a priority by 1965. President Johnson's War on Poverty promised to fund local solutions for local problems through the Office of Economic Opportunity. Groups worked in Mississippi to bring

relief while giving poor people a way to help themselves. The Delta Ministry distributed food and clothing, promoted community development, and spoke for racial reconciliation. It developed Head Start centers, rural health clinics, adult literacy classes, and citizenship education and organized self-help cooperatives. Their partner, the Medical Committee on Human Rights (MCHR), employed nurses who offered home visits and community health education, and black physicians who visited Head Start centers. The MCHR also advocated ending segregation in existing Mississippi hospitals and clinics. In 1965 SNCC activist Jesse Morris helped organize the Poor People's Corporation, which set up training and marketing for small groups that produced a variety of craft items, with participants earning income from their sales. Liberty House outlet stores opened in Jackson and New York City to sell the goods.

SCHOOL DESEGREGATION AND VOTING RIGHTS

Hosea Williams and SCLC marchers demand school desegregation in Grenada, photograph, July 14 1966. The Sovereignty Commission paid informant Edward Downing $100 for photographs like this one showing "professional agitators."

The Movement achieved more victories as the decade drew to a close. In 1964 the Civil Rights Act withheld federal funds from segregated schools. A year later Congress significantly raised public school funding to a whopping $1.3 billion. The 1965 Voting Rights Act paved the way for meaningful black participation in Mississippi elections. By 1967 Mississippi's black voters numbered 263,754, more than at any time since Reconstruction. Black candidates were elected to office. School desegregation reached a tipping point in the Supreme Court's *Alexander v. Holmes County* decision in 1969, when the Court ordered Mississippi schools to desegregate "at once."

These victories came over ongoing white opposition. Many whites attempted to get around school desegregation by sending their children to recently built private academies or by implementing freedom-of-choice plans, hoping that a few token students would be enough to satisfy desegregation orders.

TEXT FOR CHOICE OF SCHOOL FORM

(Required by § 181.46 of the Statement of Policies)

¹IF SEPARATE SCHOOLS HAVE BEEN MAINTAINED FOR OTHER THAN NEGRO AND WHITE STUDENTS, TEXT IS TO BE ADJUSTED ACCORDINGLY)

(School System Name and Office Address)

(Date sent)

CHOICE OF SCHOOL FORM

This form is provided for you to choose the school your child will attend for the coming school year. It does not matter which school the child has been attending, and it does not matter whether the school you choose was formerly a white or a Negro school. No student can be enrolled without making a choice of school. This form must either be brought to any school or mailed to the Superintendent's office at the address above by _____. If the student is 15 years old by the date of choice, or will be entering the ninth or a higher grade, either the student or his parent may make the choice.

1. Name of Child _____

   Last   First   Middle

2. Age _____

3. School and grade currently or last attended _____ Grade _____

4. School Chosen (Mark X beside school chosen)

Name of School	Grades	Location
[Here list by name, grades offered, and location each school available. For example:]		
☐ George Washington High School	8–12	Adams St., Jefferson
☐ James Madison Elementary School	1– 7	Monroe St., Jackson

This form is signed by (mark proper box):

Signature _____

Address _____

Parent ☐

Date _____

Other adult person acting as parent ☐

Student ☐

This block is to be filled in by the Superintendent's office, not by person signing.
Is student assigned to school chosen? ☐ Yes ☐ No

If not, explain: _____

U.S. GOVERNMENT PRINTING OFFICE : 1966 O—210-100

Text for Choice of School form, 1966. Between 1965 and 1969, "freedom of choice" options caused many of the state's formerly all-white schools to experience some level of desegregation. However, fewer than 1,000 black students chose all-white schools in 1965 due to ongoing harassment and violence. A year later, nearly half of the districts remained strictly segregated.

Unita Blackwell campaign poster, ca. 1967. Unita Blackwell, the first black woman to serve as mayor in Mississippi, ran for office several times before being elected mayor of Mayersville in 1976.

Legislators used gerrymandering and other electoral maneuvers to attempt to dilute the impact of black voters.

Black Voters Head to the Polls

The 1967 primary and general elections marked a huge turning point. White candidates now had to court black voters. No longer able to keep blacks from voting, whites tried to prevent them from getting elected. They redrew voting districts, created multimember districts, raised candidate filing requirements, and changed positions from elected to appointed.

Overcoming voter intimidation and legislative rule changes, twenty-two black candidates won elections in 1967. In Holmes County, Robert Clark became the first black to be elected to the state legislature in the twentieth century. In Madison County one year later, Flonzie Goodloe won her race for District 1 Election Commissioner, becoming one of the first black women to be elected to countywide office in Mississippi.

In a series of decisions from 1971 to 1977, the US Supreme Court ordered the state legislature to return to single-member districts. A year later, sixteen blacks joined Robert Clark in the state legislature. Their leadership in turn helped promote greater equality in hiring by state agencies. By 1992 Mississippi had elected more black officials (825) than any other state.

WHERE DO WE GO FROM HERE?

THE CHALLENGES OF OUR TIME

Mississippi is not the same place that it was in 1961. African Americans now work alongside white colleagues in the state legislature. Students of all races attend integrated schools from preschool to the state universities. Public facilities no longer have separate entrances or restrooms. Retail businesses wait on customers on a first-come, first-served basis. People of all races share meals at downtown restaurants. Everyone is welcome on Biloxi's beaches and at the state fair.

That does not mean that Mississippi is color-blind in the twenty-first century. Either by habit, choice, convenience, economics, or design, race continues to divide Mississippi communities. Minority populations lag behind whites in economic and educational achievement but outnumber them in Mississippi prisons. The state has made great strides, but the work of fulfilling the Constitution's promise of equal rights for all citizens remains an ongoing challenge for current and future generations to overcome.

> We have to have truthful, meaningful conversations with each other. We may not always agree, but we need to keep talking to each other.
> —Dr. Leslie-Burl McLemore, January 9, 2012

THE LONG REACH OF CIVIL RIGHTS

The legacy of the Civil Rights Movement reaches across distance and time. Many of those students who came for Freedom Summer remained politically active when they returned home. They applied lessons learned in Mississippi to environmental, women's liberation, No Nukes, and anti-war movements. The philosophies and tactics of the Civil Rights Movement served as models for activists around the world. They influenced leaders fighting apartheid in South Africa in the 1980s and were cited by activists in the Middle East during the Arab Spring.

WHAT WILL YOUR LIGHT STAND FOR?

How would you describe a Mississippi in which all people are treated equally regardless of their race? What challenges and barriers confront the state? The nation? How can we meet those challenges together?

"For me, the summer of '64 was transformational. It gave me direction and purpose and lifelong meaning. . . . I taught for 36 years, always with the understanding that teaching can be a revolutionary act. I do think it took courage for those of us who were not from Mississippi to join the struggle that summer, but it took far more courage for the African American community who had been and still is living there. That kind of constant courage is what I strive for."

—Linda Whetmore Halpern, 2010

"I think Mississippi holds promise to being almost a model in terms of what a biracial or multiracial society can achieve."

—Governor William F. Winter, *Mississippi Today*, Mississippi Public Broadcasting, October 2, 2012

"One hundred fifty years after the Emancipation Proclamation and fifty years after the March on Washington, we celebrate the spirit of our ancestors, which has allowed us to move from a nation of unborn hopes and a history of disenfranchised votes, to today's expression of a more perfect union."

—Myrlie Evers, invocation for Inauguration of President Barack Obama, January 21, 2013

"My grandfather he loved Mississippi and he used to tell me then, he'd say 'Son, the old South and Mississippi is going to rise again and this will be a fine place to be. And the day will come when you and others who love Mississippi will stay and fight. You'll stay and fight to make it right."

—REP. ROBERT G. CLARK

"The leaders in the future . . . have a definite responsibility to help, because much of what we are struggling for now will benefit them directly 10 years from now—will open up opportunities that were not open when I came along."

—MEDGAR EVERS, 1958

"Let a new earth rise. Let another world be born. Let a bloody peace be written in the sky. Let a second generation full of courage issue forth; let a people loving freedom come to growth. Let a beauty full of healing and a strength of final clenching be the pulsing in our spirits and our blood. Let the martial songs be written, let the dirges disappear. Let a race of men now rise and take control."

—FROM MARGARET WALKER, "FOR MY PEOPLE" IN *This Is My Century: New and Collected Poems* © 1989 BY MARGARET WALKER. REPRINTED BY PERMISSION OF UNIVERSITY OF GEORGIA PRESS

Acknowledgments

LIKE THE 2 MISSISSIPPI MUSEUMS, this publication is the work of many hands. I extend my sincerest gratitude to Baptist Health Systems, whose generosity made this book possible.

Four governors have supported the museum project—I want to thank Governor Phil Bryant and former governors Haley Barbour, Ronnie Musgrove, and William F. Winter. I am also grateful to the Mississippi Legislature for its generous support of the 2 Mississippi Museums. Lieutenant Governor Tate Reeves and House Speaker Philip Gunn have been strong advocates for the project, and we appreciate their leadership.

The construction project had the benefit of an exceptional team: ECD Architects and Engineers, a Joint Venture, in Consultation with the Freelon Group; Thrash Commercial Contractors Inc.; and the Bureau of Building of the Mississippi Department of Finance and Administration.

The project team created world-class exhibits and audiovisual programs, and the book draws on this exceptional work. I thank the exhibit design firms, The Design Minds Inc. and Hilferty and Associates, and the audiovisual firms, Northern Light Productions and Monadnock Media. The fabrication firms, 1220 Exhibits and Exhibit Concepts Inc., brought the exhibits to reality.

Our many scholars and advisors held the exhibits to the highest standard of scholarship and truth. I thank the Community Advisory Committee, Teacher Advisory Group, Core Scholar Committees, Mississippi Civil Rights Museum Advisory Commission, our Native American partners, and other advisors. I am grateful for their counsel and for their rigorous review. Myrlie Evers and the Veterans of the Mississippi Civil Rights Movement were invaluable partners in this process.

Vase, ceramic with glaze, decorated with ducks and waves by Walter Anderson for Shearwater Pottery, date unknown. In 1928 Peter Anderson founded Shearwater with the support of his parents, George Walter Anderson and Annette McConnell Anderson. His two younger brothers, Walter Inglis Anderson and James McConnell Anderson, joined the pottery in 1930.

I want to thank President Beverly Hogan and Tougaloo College. The College's Civil Rights Collection is housed at the Department of Archives and History, and many items from it will be exhibited in the museums. I salute this outstanding institution for its longtime leadership in civil rights and its commitment to the museum project.

We are grateful to the many generous people who have helped this department build its collection by donating thousands of artifacts and documents that allow us to tell our shared stories.

Many individual, nonprofit, and corporate donors have contributed to the museum project, and they are permanently acknowledged on the donor wall. I am grateful for their commitment and generosity. The fundraising campaign owes its success to the outstanding leadership provided by the Foundation for Mississippi History and the Foundation for the Mississippi Civil Rights Museum. The campaign was ably led by a steering committee whose members are Reuben V. Anderson, Fred Banks, Haley Fisackerly, Luke Lampton, William F. Winter, and myself. Holly Wagner was instrumental in planning and executing the fundraising campaign.

The Mississippi Department of Archives and History has worked for years to make the 2 Mississippi Museums a success. I thank my colleagues on the Board of Trustees for their leadership and the staff for their outstanding work. In particular I want to thank department directors emeritus Elbert Hilliard and H. T. Holmes, current director Katie Blount, and 2 Mississippi Museums project director Lucy Allen.

I am proud to have been part of the team that created the 2 Mississippi Museums and the book that documents this remarkable project.

KANE DITTO
President, Board of Trustees
Mississippi Department of Archives and History

Selected Bibliography

Anderson, Devery S. *Emmett Till: The Murder That Shocked the World and Propelled the Civil Rights Movement*. Jackson: University Press of Mississippi, 2015.

Arsenault, Raymond. *Freedom Riders: 1961 and the Struggle for Racial Justice*. New York: Oxford University Press, 2006.

Ballard, Michael B. *The Civil War in Mississippi: Major Campaigns and Battles*. Jackson: University Press of Mississippi, 2011.

Barbour, Haley, with Jere Nash. *America's Great Storm: Leading through Hurricane Katrina*. Jackson: University Press of Mississippi, 2015.

Barnett, James F., Jr. *Mississippi's American Indians*. Jackson: University Press of Mississippi, 2012.

Barnwell, Marion. *A Place Called Mississippi: Collected Narratives*. Jackson: University Press of Mississippi, 1997.

Barry, John M. *Rising Tide: The Great Mississippi Flood of 1927 and How It Changed America*. New York: Simon & Schuster, 1997.

Black, Patti Carr. *Art in Mississippi, 1720–1980*. Jackson: University Press of Mississippi, 1998.

Bolton, Charles C. *The Hardest Deal of All: The Battle over School Integration in Mississippi, 1870–1980*. Jackson: University Press of Mississippi, 2005.

Bond, Bradley G. *Mississippi: A Documentary History*. Jackson: University Press of Mississippi, 2005.

Brookes, Samuel O. *The First Mississippians*. Mississippi Archaeological Association, www.msarchaeology.org/maa/brookes.pdf.

Bunn, Mike, and Clay Williams. *Battle for the Southern Frontier: The Creek War and the War of 1812*. Charleston, SC: The History Press, 2008.

Busbee, Westley F., Jr. *Mississippi: A History*. Wheeling, IL: Harlan Davidson, Inc., 2005.

Carpenter, Barbara, ed. *Ethnic Heritage in Mississippi*. Jackson: University Press of Mississippi, 1992.

Carson, Clayborne. *In Struggle: SNCC and the Black Awakening of the 1960s*. Cambridge: Harvard University Press, 1981.

Chickasaw Nation. "Official Site of Chickasaw Nation." https://chickasaw.net/.

Choctaw Nation. https://www.choctawnation.com/.

Civil War Trust. http://www.civilwar.org/.

Cohen, Edward. *The Peddler's Grandson: Growing Up Jewish in Mississippi*. Jackson: University Press of Mississippi, 1999.

Connaway, John. *Fishweirs: A World Perspective with Emphasis on the Fishweirs of Mississippi*. Jackson: Mississippi Department of Archives and History, 2007.

Connaway, John M., Samuel O. Brookes, and Samuel O. McGahey. *The Denton Site: A Middle Archaic Occupation in the Northern Yazoo Basin, Mississippi*. Jackson: Mississippi Department of Archives and History, 1977.

Conway, Richard. *Democracy's Soldiers: Mississippians and Wars in the Twentieth Century*. Mississippi Oral History Program, 2002.

Crespino, Joseph. *In Search of Another Country: Mississippi and the Conservative Counterrevolution*. Princeton: Princeton University Press, 2007.

Cresswell, Stephen. *Rednecks, Redeemers, and Race: Mississippi after Reconstruction, 1877–1917*. Jackson: University Press of Mississippi, 2006.

Crosby, Emilye. *A Little Taste of Freedom: The Black Freedom Struggle in Claiborne County, Mississippi*. Chapel Hill: University of North Carolina Press, 2005.

Curry, Constance. *Silver Rights*. Chapel Hill, NC: Algonquin Books of Chapel Hill, 1995.

Dattel, Gene. *Cotton and Race in the Making of America: The Human Costs of Economic Power*. Chicago: Ivan R. Dee, 2009.

Dittmer, John. *Local People: The Struggle for Civil Rights in Mississippi*. Urbana: University of Illinois Press, 1994.

———. *The Good Doctors: The Medical Committee for Human Rights and the Struggle for Social Justice in Health Care*. New York: Bloomsbury Press, 2009.

Dougherty, Kevin. *Weapons of Mississippi*. Jackson: University Press of Mississippi, 2010.

Eaddy, Justin C. "Mississippi State Parks: The New Deal's Mixed Legacy." *Journal of Mississippi History* 65 (2003): 147–68.

Eagles, Charles W. *The Price of Defiance: James Meredith and the Integration of Ole Miss*. Chapel Hill: University of North Carolina Press, 2009.

Etheridge, Eric. *Breach of Peace: Portraits of the 1961 Mississippi Freedom Riders*. New York: Atlas & Co., 2008.

Eubanks, W. Ralph. *Ever Is a Long Time: A Journey into Mississippi's Dark Past*. New York: Basic Books, 2003.

Evers-Williams, Myrlie, with William Peters. *For Us, the Living*. Garden City, NY: Doubleday & Co., 1967.

Evers-Williams, Myrlie, and Manning Marable, eds. *The Autobiography of Medgar Evers*. New York: Basic Civitas/Harper Collins, 2005.

Galloway, Patricia. *Choctaw Genesis 1500–1700*. Lincoln: University of Nebraska Press, 1998.

Hamlin, Françoise N. *Crossroads at Clarksdale: The Black Freedom Struggle in the Mississippi Delta after World War II.* Chapel Hill: University of North Carolina Press, 2012.

Harris, William C. *The Day of the Carpetbagger: Republican Reconstruction in Mississippi.* Baton Rouge: Louisiana State University Press, 1979.

Haynes, Robert V. *The Natchez District and the American Revolution.* Jackson: University Press of Mississippi, 1976.

———. *The Mississippi Territory and the Southwest Frontier, 1795–1817.* Lexington: University Press of Kentucky, 2010.

Hendrickson, Paul. *Sons of Mississippi.* New York: Alfred A. Knopf, 2003.

Hickman, Nollie. *Mississippi Harvest: Lumbering in the Longleaf Pine Belt, 1840–1915.* Oxford: University of Mississippi, 1962.

Holsaert, Faith S., Martha Prescod Norman Noonan, Judy Richardson, Betty Garman Robinson, Jean Smith Young, and Dorothy M. Zellner, eds. *Hands on the Freedom Plow: Personal Accounts by Women in SNCC.* Urbana: University of Illinois Press, 2010.

Hudson, Charles. *The Southeastern Indians.* Knoxville: University of Tennessee Press, 1976.

Huie, William Bradford. *Three Lives for Mississippi.* New York: WCC Books, 1965.

Johnson, Mary Elizabeth. *Mississippi Quilts.* Jackson: University Press of Mississippi, 2001.

Katagiri, Yasuhiro. *The Mississippi State Sovereignty Commission: Civil Rights and States' Rights.* Jackson: University Press of Mississippi, 2001.

Kirwan, Albert D. *Revolt of the Rednecks.* Lexington: University of Kentucky Press, 1951.

Lee, Chana Kai. *For Freedom's Sake: The Life of Fannie Lou Hamer.* Urbana: University of Illinois Press, 1999.

Lemann, Nicholas. *Redemption: The Last Battle of the Civil War.* New York: Farrar, Straus and Giroux, 2006.

Loewen, James W., and Charles Sallis. *Mississippi: Conflict and Change.* New York: Pantheon Books, 1974.

Lord, Walter. *The Past That Would Not Die.* New York: Harper & Row Publishers, 1965.

Luckett, Robert E., Jr. *Joe T. Patterson and the White South's Dilemma: Evolving Resistance to Black Advancement.* Jackson: University Press of Mississippi, 2015.

Marszalek, John F. *Sherman: A Soldier's Passion for Order.* New York: Free Press, 1993.

Mason, Gilbert R., MD. *Beaches, Blood, and Ballots: A Black Doctor's Civil Rights Struggle.* Jackson: University Press of Mississippi, 2007.

McAdam, Doug. *Freedom Summer.* New York: Oxford University Press, 1988.

McLemore, Richard Aubrey, ed. *A History of Mississippi, Vol 1–2.* Hattiesburg: University & College Press of Mississippi, 1973.

McMillen, Neil R. *The Citizens' Council: Organized Resistance to the Second Reconstruction.* Urbana: University of Illinois Press, 1971.

———. *Dark Journey: Black Mississippians in the Age of Jim Crow*. Urbana: University of Illinois Press, 1989.

McRaney, Bob, Sr. *The History of Radio in Mississippi*. 1980.

Meredith, James. *Three Years in Mississippi*. Bloomington: Indiana University Press, 1966.

Mississippi History Now, an online publication of the Mississippi Historical Society. http://mshistorynow.mdah.ms.gov/.

Mississippi National Guard. http://ms.ng.mil/Pages/default.aspx.

Mississippi Rails: Mississippi's Railroad History & Heritage. http://www.msrailroads.com.

Mitchell, Dennis J. *A New History of Mississippi*. Jackson: University Press of Mississippi, 2014.

Moody, Anne. *Coming of Age in Mississippi*. New York: Doubleday, 1968.

Moore, John Hebron. *Agriculture in Ante-Bellum Mississippi*. New York: Octagon Books, 1971.

Morrison, Minion K. C. *Aaron Henry of Mississippi: Inside Agitator*. Fayetteville: University of Arkansas Press, 2015.

Nash, Jere, and Andy Taggart. *Mississippi Politics: The Struggle for Power, 1976–2008*. Jackson: University Press of Mississippi, 2009.

National Park Service. "Indian Mounds of Mississippi." http://www.nps.gov/nr/travel/mounds /intro.htm.

———. "The Modern Civil Rights Movement, 1954–1964." http://www.nps.gov/subjects/civilrights /modern-civil-rights-movement.htm.

———. "Natchez Trace Parkway." https://www.nps.gov/natr/index.htm.

———. "Southeast Archeological Center." https://www.nps.gov/seac/index.htm.

Newman, Mark. *Divine Agitators: The Delta Ministry and Civil Rights in Mississippi*. Athens: University of Georgia Press, 2004.

Newton, Michael. *The Ku Klux Klan in Mississippi: A History*. Jefferson, NC: McFarland & Company, Inc., 2010.

Nossiter, Adam. *Of Long Memory: Mississippi and the Murder of Medgar Evers*. Reading, MA: Addison-Wesley, 1994.

O'Brien, M. J. *We Shall Not Be Moved: The Jackson Woolworth's Sit-In and the Movement It Inspired*. Jackson: University Press of Mississippi, 2013.

Oshinsky, David M. *Worse Than Slavery: Parchman Farm and the Ordeal of Jim Crow Justice*. New York: Free Press, 1996.

Parker, Frank R. *Black Votes Count: Political Empowerment in Mississippi after 1965*. Chapel Hill: University of North Carolina Press, 1990.

Payne, Charles M. *I've Got the Light of Freedom: The Organizing Tradition and the Mississippi Freedom Struggle*. Berkeley: University of California Press, 2007.

Percy, William Alexander. *Lanterns on the Levee: Recollections of a Planter's Son*. Baton Rouge: Louisiana State University Press, 2006.

Rowland, Dunbar. *Encyclopedia of Mississippi History: Comprising Sketches of Counties, Towns, Events, Institutions, and Persons*. Vol. 1 and 2. Madison, WI: S.A. Brant, 1907.

Salter, John R., Jr. *Jackson, Mississippi: An American Chronicle of Struggle and Schism*. Hicksville, NY: Exposition-Banner Book, 1979.

Sansing, David G. *A Place Called Mississippi*. Lilburn, GA: Clairmont Press, 2013.

Silver, James W. *Mississippi: The Closed Society*. New York: Harcourt, Brace & World, 1963.

Skates, John R., Jr. "World War II as a Watershed in Mississippi History." *Journal of Mississippi History* 37 (1975): 131–42.

Skates, John Ray, and David G. Sansing. *Mississippi: The Study of Our State*. Brandon, MS: Walthall Publishing Company, 1993.

Smith, Timothy B. *Mississippi in the Civil War: The Home Front*. Jackson: University Press of Mississippi, 2010.

Southern Foodways Alliance. https://www.southernfoodways.org.

Sparks, Randy J. *Religion in Mississippi*. Jackson: University Press of Mississippi, 2012.

Strom, Claire. *Making Catfish Bait Out of Government Boys*. Athens: University of Georgia Press, 2009.

Sugarman, Tracy. *Stranger at the Gates: A Summer in Mississippi*. New York: Hill and Wang, 1966.

Sutherland, Elizabeth, ed. *Letters from Mississippi*. New York: McGraw-Hill Books Company, 1965.

Swain, Martha H., Elizabeth Anne Payne, and Marjorie Julian Spruill, ed. *Mississippi Women: Their Histories, Their Lives*. Athens: University of Georgia Press, 2003.

Thompson, Julius E. *Lynchings in Mississippi: A History, 1865–1965*. Jefferson, NC: McFarland & Company, Inc., 2007

Usner, Daniel H., Jr. *Indians, Settlers, and Slaves in a Frontier Exchange Economy: The Lower Mississippi Valley before 1783*. Chapel Hill: University of North Carolina Press, 1992.

Ward, Jason Morgan. *Defending White Democracy: The Making of a Segregationist Movement and the Remaking of Racial Politics, 1936–1965*. Chapel Hill: University of North Carolina Press, 2011.

Watson, Bruce. *Freedom Summer: The Savage Season That Made Mississippi Burn and Made America a Democracy*. New York: Viking, 2010.

White, Richard. *The Roots of Dependency: Subsistence, Environment, and Social Change among the Choctaws, Pawnees, and Navajos*. Lincoln: University of Nebraska Press, 1983.

Wilkerson, Isabel. *The Warmth of Other Suns: The Epic Story of America's Great Migration*. New York: Random House, 2010.

William Winter Institute for Racial Reconciliation. http://winterinstitute.org.

Williams, Michael Vinson. *Medgar Evers: Mississippi Martyr.* Fayetteville: University of Arkansas Press, 2011.

Wilson, Christine. *All Shook Up: Mississippi Roots of American Popular Music.* Jackson: Mississippi Department of Archives and History, 1995.

Wright, Richard. *Black Boy: A Record of Childhood and Youth.* New York: Harper Perennial Modern Classics, 2007.

Wyatt-Brown, Bertram. *Southern Honor: Ethics and Behavior in the Old South.* Oxford: Oxford University Press, 1982.

About the Contributors

REUBEN V. ANDERSON is a senior partner with Phelps Dunbar LLP in Jackson, Mississippi. He is a former municipal, county, and circuit judge and served as a justice on the Mississippi Supreme Court for six years. He also serves on the board of the Mississippi Department of Archives and History and is chairman of the Foundation for the Mississippi Civil Rights Museum.

HALEY BARBOUR was elected governor of Mississippi in 2003 and re-elected in 2007, completing his second term in January 2012. He served as political director of the Reagan White House in 1985–1986 and as chairman of the Republican National Committee from 1993 to 1997. He and his wife, Marsha, live in Yazoo City and have two sons and six grandchildren.

From the beginning, MYRLIE EVERS worked alongside her husband, Medgar. In the years following his assassination, she continued the pioneering work they had begun together. An author, lecturer, and educator, she was one of the first African American women to run for Congress. In 1995 she was elected chairperson of the NAACP and helped rebuild and restore the national reputation of the organization. In 1989 she founded the Medgar Evers Institute, with the initial goal of preserving and advancing the legacy of Medgar Evers's life's work. Upon the commemoration of the fiftieth anniversary of his assassination, and recognizing the international leadership role of Myrlie Evers, the Institute's board of directors changed the organization's name to the Medgar and Myrlie Evers Institute. She currently serves as chairman of the Institute.

JOHN E. FLEMING, PhD, has been a museum director since 1980, serving as the founding director of the National Afro-American Museum and Cultural

Center in Wilberforce, Ohio, and the National Underground Railroad Freedom Center in Cincinnati, Ohio. He has published numerous articles on African American history and culture and has served as president of the Association of African American Museums, the Ohio Museums Association, the Association for the Study of African American Life and History, and is now vice president and president-elect of the Association for State and Local History.

DENNIS J. MITCHELL, PhD, is the author of the *New History of Mississippi* and editor of the *Journal of Mississippi History*, was assistant director of the Mississippi Humanities Council for several years, and taught at Jackson State University and Mississippi State University for over thirty. He has written several books ranging from British and world history to an account of Meridian's Grand Opera House. He is professor emeritus at Mississippi State University.

WILLIAM F. WINTER served as governor of Mississippi from 1980 to 1984. Prior to that he had been elected to the offices of state representative, state tax collector, state treasurer, and lieutenant governor. He has been chairman of the Southern Regional Education Board, the Appalachian Regional Commission, the Southern Growth Policies Board, the Commission on the Future of the South, the National Civic League, the Kettering Foundation, the Foundation for the Mid South, and the Mississippi Department of Archives and History.

KANE DITTO is the owner of StateStreet Group, LLC, a real estate development company which he started in 1971. He served as mayor of the City of Jackson from July 1989 until July 1997. He was elected to the Mississippi House of Representatives from District 66, where he served from 1987 to 1989. He practiced law for eighteen years with Watkins Ludlam Winter & Stennis in Jackson, where he was managing partner of the firm for five years. He now serves as president of the board of trustees of the Mississippi Department of Archives and History and vice-chairman of the board of trustees of Baptist Health Systems. He also serves on the boards of the Mississippi Delta National Heritage Area Partnership and Mississippi Chapter of the Juvenile Diabetes Research Foundation.

Index

Page numbers in **bold** indicate illustrations.